Diabetic Diet Cookbook for Beginners

Discover Tasty Low-Sugar and Low-Carb Recipes to Support Blood Sugar Balance, Promote Wellness and Enjoy a Healthier, Happier Lifestyle Every Day!

Reto Teufel

© Copyright 2024 - Reto Teufel - All rights reserved

The information provided in this book is intended for educational and informational purposes only. While the recipes and nutritional guidelines shared here are based on well-established dietary principles, they are not a substitute for professional medical advice, diagnosis, or treatment. The content is not meant to be used as medical guidance, and it is essential that you consult with a healthcare professional before implementing any significant dietary changes.

If you have any pre-existing medical conditions, food allergies, or dietary restrictions, please seek advice from a qualified healthcare provider, nutritionist, or dietitian. Each individual's health situation is unique, and what works for one person may not be suitable for another. Personalized nutritional advice tailored to your specific needs and medical history is always recommended.

The author and publisher have made every effort to ensure that the information provided in this book is accurate and up-to-date at the time of publication. However, nutritional science is constantly evolving, and new information may emerge that could change the understanding of dietary practices. Therefore, the author and publisher cannot be held responsible for any errors or omissions or for any consequences that arise from the use of the material provided.

By following the recipes and suggestions in this book, you assume full responsibility for any risks associated with dietary changes, and you agree that the author and publisher shall not be held liable for any loss, damage, or adverse effects related to the use or misuse of the information provided. Always read ingredient labels carefully and be aware of any potential allergens when preparing meals.

In summary, this book is designed to inspire and guide, but it should not be relied upon as a sole resource for managing specific health conditions. Consult a professional for tailored advice, and always prioritize your individual health needs.

Table of Contents

1. Introduction to diabetic diet 7
   1.1 Understanding diabetes and its types 8
   1.2 The role of macronutrients in a diabetic diet 10
   1.3 How to read and understand food labels 11
2. Understanding your ingredients 14
   2.1 Carbohydrates and fiber: the essentials 15
   2.2 Proteins: building a balanced diet 17
   2.3 Fats and oils: choosing the right types 18
3. Breakfasts to start your day 21
   3.1 Oatmeal with chia and berries 21
   3.2 Spinach and feta egg muffins 21
   3.3 Almond butter smoothie 22
   3.4 Cottage cheese and peach parfait 23
   3.5 Turkey and avocado wrap 23
   3.6 Quinoa and apple breakfast bowl 24
   3.7 Greek yogurt with nuts and honey 25
   3.8 Tofu scramble with vegetables 25
   3.9 Buckwheat pancakes 26
   3.10 Chia pudding with coconut milk 27
   3.11 Smoked salmon and cream cheese bagel 27
   3.12 Kale and sweet potato hash 28
   3.13 Blueberry and almond oat bars 28
   3.14 Ricotta and pear toast 29
   3.15 Vegetable omelette 30
   3.16 Protein-packed breakfast tacos 30
   3.17 Banana and walnut bread 31
   3.18 Green detox smoothie 32
4. Nutritious and satisfying lunches 33
   4.1 Turkey and avocado wrap 33
   4.2 Quinoa and black bean salad 34
   4.3 Grilled chicken caesar salad 34
   4.4 Vegetable lentil soup 35
   4.5 Spinach and feta stuffed chicken 36
   4.6 Roasted vegetable and hummus wrap 36
   4.7 Tuna salad stuffed tomatoes 37
   4.8 Broccoli and cheddar stuffed potatoes 38

- 4.9 Asian chicken salad ... 39
- 4.10 Mediterranean chickpea wrap ... 39
- 4.11 Zucchini noodle and shrimp bowl ... 40
- 4.12 Turkey chili ... 41
- 4.13 Egg salad on rye ... 42
- 4.14 Balsamic chicken and roasted vegetable salad ... 43
- 4.15 Smoked salmon and cream cheese bagel ... 43
- 4.16 Beef and vegetable stir-fry ... 44
- 4.17 Caprese salad with grilled chicken ... 45
- 4.18 Butternut squash soup ... 45

5. Delicious diabetic-friendly dinners ... 47
- 5.1 Grilled chicken with quinoa salad ... 47
- 5.2 Turkey and spinach stuffed peppers ... 48
- 5.3 Baked salmon with steamed broccoli ... 49
- 5.4 Vegetarian chili ... 49
- 5.5 Beef and vegetable stir-fry ... 50
- 5.6 Lentil and mushroom stew ... 51
- 5.7 Cauliflower rice and shrimp bowl ... 52
- 5.8 Spaghetti squash with turkey meatballs ... 53
- 5.9 Grilled vegetable platter with herb dressing ... 53
- 5.10 Pork tenderloin with apple cider glaze ... 54
- 5.11 Zucchini noodles with basil pesto ... 55
- 5.12 Chicken tikka masala with cauliflower ... 56
- 5.13 Eggplant and chickpea tagine ... 56
- 5.14 Baked cod with olive tapenade ... 57
- 5.15 Tofu and vegetable curry ... 58
- 5.16 Stuffed acorn squash ... 59
- 5.17 Chicken and barley soup ... 60
- 5.18 Roasted turkey with garlic green beans ... 60

6. Salads full of flavor ... 62
- 6.1 Spinach and strawberry salad ... 62
- 6.2 Grilled chicken caesar with kale ... 62
- 6.3 Mediterranean chickpea salad ... 63
- 6.4 Quinoa and black bean salad ... 64
- 6.5 Beetroot and goat cheese salad ... 64
- 6.6 Asian tofu salad ... 65
- 6.7 Turkey and cranberry salad ... 66
- 6.8 Cucumber and dill salad ... 67
- 6.9 Avocado and shrimp salad ... 67

    6.10   Roasted vegetable salad 68

    6.11   Smoked salmon and arugula salad 69

    6.12   Watermelon and feta salad 69

    6.13   Tuna and white bean salad 70

    6.14   Broccoli and almond salad 71

    6.15   Pear and blue cheese salad 71

    6.16   Buffalo chicken salad 72

    6.17   Greek salad with grilled lamb 73

    6.18   Carrot and raisin salad 73

7. Soothing and hearty soups 75

    7.1   Classic chicken noodle soup 75

    7.2   Creamy tomato basil soup 76

    7.3   Lentil and spinach soup 76

    7.4   Beef and barley soup 77

    7.5   Butternut squash and ginger soup 78

    7.6   Turkey and vegetable soup 79

    7.7   Cauliflower and leek soup 79

    7.8   Miso soup with tofu and seaweed 80

    7.9   Minestrone with whole grain pasta 81

    7.10   Spicy black bean soup 82

    7.11   Pumpkin and sage soup 82

    7.12   Chicken tortilla soup 83

    7.13   White bean and kale soup 84

    7.14   Carrot and coriander soup 85

    7.15   Pea and mint soup 85

    7.16   Mushroom and thyme soup 86

    7.17   Asian chicken and ginger broth 87

    7.18   Split pea and ham soup 88

8. Snacks for energy and health 89

    8.1   Almond and pumpkin seed mix 89

    8.2   Chia and berry yogurt parfait 89

    8.3   Cucumber hummus bites 90

    8.4   Avocado and egg salad 91

    8.5   Spinach and feta stuffed mushrooms 91

    8.6   Low-carb blueberry muffins 92

    8.7   Spicy roasted chickpeas 93

    8.8   Coconut and almond energy balls 93

    8.9   Turkey and cheese roll-ups 94

    8.10   Green apple and peanut butter slices 95

- 8.11 Flaxseed and walnut crackers 95
- 8.12 Zucchini and parmesan chips 96
- 8.13 Bell pepper and guacamole boats 96
- 8.14 Cottage cheese and cherry tomatoes 97
- 8.15 Smoked salmon and cream cheese cucumber rolls 98
- 8.16 Baked kale chips 98
- 8.17 Peanut butter and banana smoothie 99
- 8.18 Grilled vegetable kebabs 99
9. 4-week meal plan for diabetes management 101
10. Conclusion: embracing a healthy lifestyle 105
    - 10.1 Reflecting on your journey 106
    - 10.2 Staying motivated in your diet journey 108
    - 10.3 Integrating healthy habits into daily life 109

1. Introduction to diabetic diet

Diabetes is a chronic condition that affects millions of people worldwide, and its management is crucial for maintaining a healthy lifestyle. One of the most effective ways to manage diabetes is through a carefully planned diet. This chapter provides an in-depth overview of diabetes, focusing on the importance of diet in managing blood sugar levels. It will introduce the basics of a diabetic diet, discuss the role of carbohydrates, proteins, and fats, and explain how to read food labels effectively. Understanding diabetes begins with recognizing its different types. Type 1 diabetes is an autoimmune condition where the body attacks insulin-producing cells in the pancreas, leading to little or no insulin production.

Type 2 diabetes, which is more common, occurs when the body becomes resistant to insulin or when the pancreas does not produce enough insulin. Gestational diabetes occurs during pregnancy and usually resolves after childbirth but increases the risk of developing Type 2 diabetes later in life. Regardless of the type, managing diabetes involves maintaining blood sugar levels within a target range, and diet plays a pivotal role in this management.

A diabetic diet is not about deprivation but about making healthier food choices that help control blood sugar levels. The cornerstone of a diabetic diet is understanding the role of macronutrients: carbohydrates, proteins, and fats. Carbohydrates have the most significant impact on blood sugar levels because they are broken down into glucose, which enters the bloodstream. Therefore, monitoring carbohydrate intake is essential. Carbohydrates are found in fruits, vegetables, grains, legumes, and dairy products. However, not all carbohydrates are created equal. Simple carbohydrates, such as those found in sugary snacks and beverages, cause rapid spikes in blood sugar levels, while complex carbohydrates, found in whole grains, vegetables, and legumes, are digested more slowly and have a more gradual impact on blood sugar. Fiber, a type of carbohydrate, is particularly beneficial for people with diabetes as it slows the absorption of sugar and helps improve blood sugar levels. Foods high in fiber include vegetables, fruits, whole grains, and legumes. Incorporating fiber-rich foods into your diet can help you feel full longer, aiding in weight management, which is crucial for managing diabetes.

Proteins are another essential component of a diabetic diet. They have little effect on blood sugar levels and can help you feel full and satisfied, reducing the likelihood of overeating. Good sources of protein include lean meats, poultry, fish, eggs, dairy products, legumes, and nuts. It's important to choose lean protein sources to avoid excessive intake of saturated fats, which can increase the risk of heart disease, a common complication of diabetes. Fats are also an important part of a balanced diet, but the type of fat consumed matters significantly. Unsaturated fats, found in foods like avocados, nuts, seeds, and olive oil, can help improve blood cholesterol levels and reduce inflammation. Saturated fats, found in red meat, butter, and full-fat dairy products, should be limited as they can raise blood cholesterol levels and increase the risk of heart disease. Trans fats, often found in processed and fried foods, should be avoided altogether as they are harmful to heart health.

Reading and understanding food labels is a crucial skill for managing a diabetic diet. Food labels provide information about the nutritional content of a product, including the amount of carbohydrates, proteins, fats, and fiber it contains. When reading food labels, pay attention to the serving size, as the nutritional information provided is based on a specific portion. It's easy to consume more than the recommended serving size, which can lead to higher intake of carbohydrates and calories. The total carbohydrate content on the label includes sugars, complex carbohydrates, and fiber. To manage blood sugar levels effectively, focus on the total carbohydrate content rather than just the sugar content. Additionally, look for foods with higher fiber content, as fiber helps regulate blood sugar levels. The ingredient list on food labels can also provide valuable information. Ingredients are listed in descending order by weight, so the first few ingredients make up the majority of the product. Look for whole foods and avoid products with added sugars and unhealthy fats. Ingredients like high-fructose corn syrup, hydrogenated oils, and artificial additives should be minimized.

Incorporating these principles into your daily diet can help you manage diabetes effectively. Start by planning balanced meals that include a variety of nutrient-dense foods. For breakfast, consider options like oatmeal with chia and berries, which provides a good balance of complex carbohydrates, fiber, and protein. Spinach and feta egg muffins are another excellent choice, offering protein and vegetables to start your day. For lunch, a turkey and avocado wrap provides lean protein and healthy fats, while a quinoa and black bean salad offers a combination of complex carbohydrates, fiber, and protein. Dinner options like grilled chicken with quinoa salad or baked salmon with steamed broccoli provide balanced meals that support blood sugar management. Snacks are also an important part of a diabetic diet, helping to maintain blood sugar levels between meals. Choose nutrient-dense snacks like almond and pumpkin seed mix, chia and berry yogurt parfait, or cucumber hummus bites. These snacks provide a good balance of protein, healthy fats, and fiber, helping to keep you satisfied and your blood sugar levels stable.

In conclusion, managing diabetes through diet involves understanding the role of macronutrients, making informed food choices, and reading food labels effectively. By incorporating a variety of nutrient-dense foods into your meals and snacks, you can maintain stable blood sugar levels and improve your overall health. Remember, a diabetic diet is not about restriction but about making healthier choices that support your well-being. With the right knowledge and tools, you can take control of your diabetes and enjoy a balanced, nutritious diet.

1.1 Understanding diabetes and its types

Diabetes is a chronic condition that affects millions of people worldwide, and understanding its various types is crucial for effective management, particularly through dietary choices. There are three primary types of diabetes: Type 1, Type 2, and gestational diabetes. Each type has unique characteristics and implications for the body, and diet plays a pivotal role in managing these conditions.

Type 1 diabetes, often diagnosed in children and young adults, is an autoimmune condition where the body's immune system mistakenly attacks and destroys insulin-producing beta cells in the pancreas. Without insulin, glucose cannot enter cells and remains in the bloodstream, leading to high blood sugar levels. Individuals with Type 1 diabetes must rely on insulin therapy for survival. Diet is essential in managing Type 1 diabetes as it helps regulate blood sugar levels and prevent complications. For example, a balanced diet rich in whole grains, lean proteins, healthy fats, and plenty of fruits and vegetables can help maintain stable blood sugar levels. Carbohydrate counting is a common strategy used by those with Type 1 diabetes to match insulin doses with carbohydrate intake, ensuring better blood sugar control.

Type 2 diabetes is the most common form of diabetes, accounting for about 90-95% of all diabetes cases. It typically develops in adults over the age of 45, although it is increasingly seen in younger individuals due to rising obesity rates. Type 2 diabetes occurs when the body becomes resistant to insulin or when the pancreas fails to produce enough insulin. This leads to elevated blood sugar levels, which can cause various health complications over time, such as heart disease, kidney damage, and nerve damage. Diet plays a critical role in managing Type 2 diabetes. A diet low in refined sugars and high in fiber can help improve insulin sensitivity and lower blood sugar levels. For instance, incorporating foods like whole grains, legumes, nuts, seeds, and non-starchy vegetables into meals can provide sustained energy and prevent blood sugar spikes. Additionally, portion control and mindful eating practices can aid in weight management, which is crucial for individuals with Type 2 diabetes.

Gestational diabetes occurs during pregnancy and affects how the body processes glucose. It typically develops around the 24th week of pregnancy and usually resolves after childbirth. However, women who have had gestational diabetes are at a higher risk of developing Type 2 diabetes later in life. Managing gestational diabetes involves monitoring blood sugar levels, eating a balanced diet, and engaging in regular physical activity. A diet rich in complex carbohydrates, lean proteins, and healthy fats can help maintain stable blood sugar levels and support the health of both the mother and the baby. For example, meals that include whole grains, lean meats, fish, eggs, dairy products, and plenty of vegetables can provide essential nutrients without causing significant blood sugar fluctuations.

Research has shown that diet is a powerful tool in managing all types of diabetes. For instance, a study published in the journal "Diabetes Care" found that a Mediterranean diet, which is high in fruits, vegetables, whole grains, and healthy fats, can significantly improve blood sugar control and reduce the risk of cardiovascular complications in individuals with diabetes. Another study published in "The Lancet" demonstrated that a low-carbohydrate, high-protein diet could lead to better glycemic control and weight loss in people with Type 2 diabetes.

Case studies also highlight the importance of diet in diabetes management. Take the example of John, a 50-year-old man diagnosed with Type 2 diabetes. John struggled with high blood sugar levels and weight gain for years. After consulting with a dietitian, he adopted a low-carb, high-fiber diet and started incorporating regular physical activity into his routine. Within six months, John lost 30 pounds, and his blood sugar levels stabilized. He reported feeling more energetic and less reliant on medication to manage his diabetes.

Similarly, Sarah, a 35-year-old woman with gestational diabetes, managed her condition through dietary changes and regular exercise. By focusing on nutrient-dense foods and avoiding sugary snacks, Sarah maintained healthy blood sugar levels throughout her pregnancy and gave birth to a healthy baby. Her experience underscores the importance of diet in managing gestational diabetes and preventing long-term health issues.

In conclusion, understanding the different types of diabetes and the role of diet in managing these conditions is essential for anyone affected by this chronic disease. Whether it's Type 1, Type 2, or gestational diabetes, a well-balanced diet tailored to individual needs can significantly improve blood sugar control, prevent complications, and enhance overall well-being. By making informed dietary choices and adopting a healthy lifestyle, individuals with diabetes can lead fulfilling lives and reduce the risk of long-term health problems.

1.2 The role of macronutrients in a diabetic diet

In understanding the role of macronutrients in a diabetic diet, it is crucial to delve deeply into the significance of carbohydrates, proteins, and fats, and how they can be balanced to maintain stable blood sugar levels. Carbohydrates, often the most scrutinized macronutrient in a diabetic diet, are the body's primary source of energy. They are broken down into glucose, which directly impacts blood sugar levels. For someone like Sarah, who is newly diagnosed with Type 2 diabetes, understanding the different types of carbohydrates—simple and complex—is essential. Simple carbohydrates, found in foods like sugary snacks and sodas, are quickly absorbed by the body, leading to rapid spikes in blood sugar. In contrast, complex carbohydrates, found in whole grains, vegetables, and legumes, are digested more slowly, resulting in a gradual increase in blood sugar levels. This slow digestion process is beneficial for maintaining stable blood sugar levels throughout the day.

To illustrate, consider the difference between consuming a slice of white bread versus a slice of whole grain bread. White bread, a source of simple carbohydrates, can cause a quick surge in blood sugar, whereas whole grain bread, rich in complex carbohydrates and fiber, leads to a more controlled release of glucose into the bloodstream. Research supports that diets high in fiber, particularly soluble fiber found in oats, beans, and certain fruits, can improve blood sugar control and reduce the risk of cardiovascular disease, a common complication of diabetes. Therefore, Sarah should aim to incorporate high-fiber foods into her meals, such as oatmeal with chia seeds and berries for breakfast or a quinoa and black bean salad for lunch.

Proteins play a vital role in a diabetic diet by providing the necessary building blocks for body tissues and aiding in muscle repair and growth. They also have a minimal impact on blood sugar levels, making them a safe and satisfying choice for diabetics. Lean protein sources, such as chicken, turkey, fish, tofu, and legumes, should be prioritized. For instance, a grilled chicken Caesar salad or a spinach and feta stuffed chicken can be both nutritious and delicious options for Sarah's lunch or dinner. Additionally, incorporating plant-based proteins like lentils and chickpeas can offer a variety of nutrients and help in maintaining a balanced diet.

Fats, often misunderstood, are essential for overall health and can be included in a diabetic diet when chosen wisely. Healthy fats, such as those found in avocados, nuts, seeds, and olive oil, can help improve blood lipid levels and provide satiety, reducing the likelihood of overeating. For example, a Mediterranean chickpea wrap with a drizzle of olive oil or a snack of avocado and egg salad can be excellent choices. It is important to limit saturated fats found in red meat and full-fat dairy products, as well as trans fats found in processed foods, as these can increase the risk of heart disease.

Balancing these macronutrients involves not only choosing the right types but also understanding portion sizes and meal timing. For Sarah, meal planning can be a powerful tool in managing her diabetes. By preparing meals ahead of time, she can ensure that each meal contains a balance of carbohydrates, proteins, and fats. For instance, a dinner of baked salmon with steamed broccoli and a side of quinoa provides a well-rounded meal with complex carbohydrates, lean protein, and healthy fats. Additionally, spacing meals evenly throughout the day can help prevent blood sugar spikes and crashes. Eating smaller, more frequent meals can be particularly beneficial for maintaining energy levels and blood sugar stability.

Case studies have shown that individuals who follow a balanced diet with appropriate macronutrient distribution experience better blood sugar control and overall health outcomes. For example, a study published in the American Journal of Clinical Nutrition found that participants who consumed a diet high in complex carbohydrates and fiber, moderate in protein, and low in unhealthy fats had significantly improved glycemic control compared to those on a standard diet. This evidence underscores the importance of making informed dietary choices and highlights the benefits of a well-balanced diabetic diet.

In practical terms, Sarah can start by creating a weekly meal plan that includes a variety of foods from each macronutrient group. Breakfast options might include a spinach and feta egg muffin or a cottage cheese and peach parfait, both of which provide a good balance of protein and carbohydrates. For lunch, she could enjoy a turkey and avocado wrap or a quinoa and black bean salad, incorporating lean proteins and complex carbohydrates. Dinner could feature dishes like grilled chicken with quinoa salad or baked salmon with steamed broccoli, ensuring a mix of healthy fats, proteins, and carbohydrates. Snacks such as almond and pumpkin seed mix or cucumber hummus bites can help keep her blood sugar levels stable between meals.

Understanding food labels is another critical aspect of managing a diabetic diet. Sarah should look for foods that are high in fiber and low in added sugars and unhealthy fats. Paying attention to serving sizes and the total carbohydrate content can help her make better choices. For instance, when choosing a snack bar, she should opt for one with whole grains and nuts, and minimal added sugars. Reading labels carefully can also help her avoid hidden sugars and unhealthy fats that can sabotage her efforts to maintain stable blood sugar levels.

In conclusion, the role of macronutrients in a diabetic diet cannot be overstated. By focusing on complex carbohydrates, lean proteins, and healthy fats, Sarah can create meals that not only help manage her blood sugar levels but also provide the nutrients her body needs to thrive. Meal planning, understanding food labels, and making informed choices are key strategies in achieving a balanced diet. With dedication and the right knowledge, Sarah can navigate the complexities of diabetic nutrition and enjoy a variety of delicious and nutritious meals that support her health and well-being.

1.3 How to read and understand food labels

Reading and understanding food labels is a crucial skill for anyone managing diabetes, as it empowers individuals to make informed dietary choices that can significantly impact their blood sugar levels and overall health. Food labels provide essential information about the nutritional content of packaged foods, helping consumers determine whether a product fits within their dietary guidelines. For Sarah, a dedicated mother and high school teacher recently diagnosed with Type 2 diabetes, mastering the art of reading food labels is a vital step toward managing her condition effectively and ensuring the well-being of her family.

When examining food labels, one of the first things to look for is the serving size. The serving size listed on the label is the amount of food that the nutritional information pertains to. It is important to note that the serving size may not always reflect the portion size that one typically consumes. For instance, a bag of chips might list a serving size as one ounce, but it is easy to consume several ounces in one sitting. Understanding the serving size helps Sarah accurately gauge how much of each nutrient she is consuming and adjust her portions accordingly.

Next, Sarah should pay close attention to the total carbohydrate content. Carbohydrates have the most significant impact on blood sugar levels, so monitoring their intake is essential for diabetes management. The total carbohydrate content includes all types of carbohydrates present in the food, such as sugars, starches, and fiber. It is often broken down into subcategories like dietary fiber and sugars. Dietary fiber is beneficial for blood sugar control as it slows down the absorption of sugar into the bloodstream. Therefore, foods high in fiber are generally better choices for people with diabetes. For example, a high-fiber cereal might list 30 grams of total carbohydrates, with 10 grams of dietary fiber, resulting in a net carbohydrate content of 20 grams.

The glycemic index (GI) is another important factor to consider. The GI measures how quickly a carbohydrate-containing food raises blood sugar levels. Foods with a high GI cause rapid spikes in blood sugar, while those with a low GI result in a slower, more gradual increase. Although the GI is not always listed on food labels, Sarah can use online resources or reference guides to determine the GI of common foods. Choosing low-GI foods, such as whole grains, legumes, and non-starchy vegetables, can help Sarah maintain more stable blood sugar levels.

In addition to carbohydrates, Sarah should also examine the fat content on food labels. Not all fats are created equal, and understanding the different types of fats can help her make healthier choices. Saturated fats and trans fats are known to increase the risk of heart disease, which is a common complication of diabetes. Therefore, it is advisable to limit the intake of these fats. Instead, Sarah should look for foods that contain healthy fats, such as monounsaturated and polyunsaturated fats, which can be found in nuts, seeds, avocados, and olive oil. For example, a salad dressing might list 15 grams of total fat, with 2 grams of saturated fat and 0 grams of trans fat, indicating that it contains healthier fats.

Protein content is another key component to consider. Protein is essential for building and repairing tissues and can also help stabilize blood sugar levels by slowing down the absorption of carbohydrates. Foods high in protein can be particularly beneficial for people with diabetes. When reading food labels, Sarah should look for lean sources of protein, such as poultry, fish, beans, and low-fat dairy products. For instance, a serving of Greek yogurt might contain 15 grams of protein, making it a good choice for a balanced snack.

Sodium content is also important to monitor, as excessive sodium intake can lead to high blood pressure, another common issue for people with diabetes. The American Heart Association recommends consuming no more than 2,300 milligrams of sodium per day, with an ideal limit of 1,500 milligrams for most adults. When reading food labels, Sarah should aim to choose products with lower sodium content to help manage her blood pressure. For example, a can of soup might list 800 milligrams of sodium per serving, which is relatively high, so she might opt for a low-sodium version instead.

In addition to these key nutrients, Sarah should also be aware of other labeling terms that can provide valuable information. Terms like "sugar-free," "low-fat," and "reduced-sodium" can be helpful, but it is important to understand what they mean. "Sugar-free" means that the product contains less than 0.5 grams of sugar per serving, but it may still contain carbohydrates that can affect blood sugar levels. "Low-fat" means that the product contains 3 grams or less of fat per serving, but it is essential to check for added sugars that might be used to compensate for the reduced fat content. "Reduced-sodium" means that the product contains at least 25% less sodium than the regular version, but it may still be high in sodium overall.

Understanding ingredient lists is another critical aspect of reading food labels. Ingredients are listed in descending order by weight, so the first few ingredients are the most prominent in the product. Sarah should look for whole, unprocessed ingredients and be cautious of products with long lists of unfamiliar or artificial ingredients. For example, a whole grain bread with ingredients like whole wheat flour, water, and yeast is a better choice than one with enriched flour, high fructose corn syrup, and numerous additives.

Case studies and research further highlight the importance of reading food labels for diabetes management. A study published in the Journal of the Academy of Nutrition and Dietetics found that individuals who frequently read food labels had better dietary habits and improved glycemic control compared to those who did not. Another study in Diabetes Care demonstrated that label-reading skills were associated with lower body mass index (BMI) and reduced risk of obesity, which is a significant risk factor for Type 2 diabetes.

For Sarah, incorporating these label-reading strategies into her daily routine can make a substantial difference in her diabetes management. By carefully selecting foods that align with her dietary needs, she can create nutritious and enjoyable meals for herself and her family. For instance, when shopping for breakfast cereals, she can compare labels to find options with higher fiber content and lower added sugars. When choosing snacks, she can opt for nuts and seeds with healthy fats and protein instead of processed snacks high in saturated fats and sodium.

In conclusion, reading and understanding food labels is an essential skill for anyone managing diabetes, including Sarah. By paying attention to serving sizes, carbohydrate content, glycemic index, fat types, protein levels, sodium content, and ingredient lists, she can make informed dietary choices that support her health goals. This knowledge empowers her to navigate the complexities of diabetic nutrition, overcome challenges, and create a balanced, enjoyable diet that benefits her entire family. Through practice and persistence, Sarah can master the art of label reading, leading to improved diabetes management and a healthier, more fulfilling life.

2. Understanding your ingredients

Understanding your ingredients is a fundamental aspect of mastering a diabetic diet, and this chapter aims to provide a comprehensive guide to the essential ingredients that are particularly beneficial for managing diabetes. By delving into various food groups, we will highlight the nutritional benefits of specific foods, offer tips on selecting the best quality ingredients, and provide practical advice on storing them to maintain their freshness and nutritional value. Let's begin with carbohydrates and fiber, which are crucial components of a diabetic diet. Carbohydrates are the body's primary source of energy, but not all carbs are created equal. Complex carbohydrates, such as whole grains, legumes, and vegetables, are digested more slowly, leading to a gradual rise in blood sugar levels.

This slow digestion is beneficial for people with diabetes as it helps maintain stable blood sugar levels. Whole grains like brown rice, quinoa, barley, and oats are excellent choices. They are rich in fiber, which not only aids in digestion but also helps regulate blood sugar levels. When selecting whole grains, look for products labeled "100% whole grain" or "whole wheat" to ensure you are getting the full nutritional benefits. Store these grains in airtight containers in a cool, dry place to prevent them from becoming rancid.

Fiber is another essential component of a diabetic diet. It helps slow down the absorption of sugar, which can prevent spikes in blood glucose levels. Foods high in fiber include fruits, vegetables, legumes, and whole grains. Incorporating a variety of these foods into your diet can help you meet your daily fiber needs. For instance, apples, berries, and pears are excellent fruit choices, while vegetables like broccoli, Brussels sprouts, and carrots are high in fiber. When selecting fruits and vegetables, choose fresh, seasonal produce whenever possible. Store fruits in the refrigerator to keep them fresh longer, and keep vegetables in the crisper drawer to maintain their crispness and nutritional value.

Proteins are the building blocks of a balanced diet and play a crucial role in managing diabetes. Lean proteins, such as chicken, turkey, fish, and plant-based proteins like tofu and legumes, are excellent choices. These proteins are low in saturated fat, which is important for heart health, especially for people with diabetes who are at a higher risk of cardiovascular disease. When selecting meats, opt for cuts labeled "lean" or "extra lean," and choose skinless poultry to reduce fat intake. Fish, particularly fatty fish like salmon, mackerel, and sardines, are rich in omega-3 fatty acids, which have anti-inflammatory properties and can help improve heart health. Store meats and fish in the coldest part of your refrigerator and use them within a few days of purchase or freeze them for longer storage. Plant-based proteins, such as beans, lentils, and chickpeas, are also excellent sources of protein and fiber. These legumes can be stored in a cool, dry place and should be soaked before cooking to reduce cooking time and improve digestibility.

Fats and oils are another important consideration in a diabetic diet. While it is essential to limit saturated and trans fats, healthy fats, such as those found in avocados, nuts, seeds, and olive oil, can be beneficial. These fats can help improve cholesterol levels and provide essential fatty acids that the body needs. When selecting oils, choose those that are labeled "extra virgin" or "cold-pressed" to ensure you are getting the highest quality product. Store oils in a cool, dark place to prevent them from becoming rancid. Nuts and seeds, such as almonds, walnuts, chia seeds, and flaxseeds, are also excellent sources of healthy fats and can be stored in airtight containers in the refrigerator to maintain their freshness.

Dairy products can be included in a diabetic diet, but it is important to choose low-fat or fat-free options to reduce saturated fat intake. Greek yogurt, cottage cheese, and milk are good choices. Greek yogurt, in particular, is high in protein and can be used in a variety of dishes, from smoothies to savory dips. When selecting dairy products, look for those that are labeled "low-fat" or "fat-free" and check the ingredient list for added sugars. Store dairy products in the coldest part of your refrigerator and use them by the expiration date to ensure freshness.

Sweeteners are another important consideration for people with diabetes. While it is best to limit added sugars, there are several alternative sweeteners that can be used in moderation. Stevia, erythritol, and monk fruit are natural sweeteners that do not raise blood sugar levels and can be used in baking and cooking. When selecting sweeteners, choose those that are labeled "natural" and avoid those with added fillers or artificial ingredients. Store sweeteners in a cool, dry place to maintain their quality.

Herbs and spices are a great way to add flavor to your meals without adding extra calories or sodium. Fresh herbs, such as basil, cilantro, and parsley, can be stored in the refrigerator, while dried herbs and spices should be kept in a cool, dark place. Spices like cinnamon, turmeric, and ginger have anti-inflammatory properties and can be beneficial for people with diabetes. When selecting herbs and spices, choose those that are fresh and fragrant, and store them properly to maintain their potency.

In conclusion, understanding your ingredients is crucial for managing diabetes effectively. By choosing high-quality, nutrient-dense foods and storing them properly, you can create delicious and nutritious meals that support your health and well-being. Incorporating a variety of whole grains, high-fiber foods, lean proteins, healthy fats, low-fat dairy, natural sweeteners, and flavorful herbs and spices into your diet can help you maintain stable blood sugar levels and improve your overall health. Remember to read food labels carefully, select fresh, seasonal produce, and store your ingredients properly to ensure you are getting the most nutritional value from your food. With these tips, you can feel confident in your food choices and enjoy a healthy, balanced diet that supports your diabetes management goals.

2.1 Carbohydrates and fiber: the essentials

Carbohydrates and dietary fiber play a pivotal role in the management of diabetes, and understanding their impact on blood sugar levels is essential for anyone looking to maintain a balanced and healthy diet. Carbohydrates, often referred to as carbs, are one of the primary macronutrients found in our diet. They are the body's main source of energy, but not all carbohydrates are created equal. For individuals with diabetes, it is crucial to distinguish between simple and complex carbohydrates and to prioritize the latter for better blood sugar control.

Simple carbohydrates, or simple sugars, are found in foods such as candies, sodas, and baked goods made with white flour. These carbs are quickly broken down by the body, leading to rapid spikes in blood sugar levels. On the other hand, complex carbohydrates are found in whole grains, legumes, and vegetables. These carbs are digested more slowly, resulting in a gradual release of glucose into the bloodstream, which helps maintain stable blood sugar levels. For Sarah, our dedicated mother and high school teacher, incorporating complex carbohydrates into her diet can make a significant difference in managing her Type 2 diabetes.

One of the key benefits of complex carbohydrates is their high fiber content. Dietary fiber, a type of carbohydrate that the body cannot digest, is found in plant-based foods such as fruits, vegetables, whole grains, and legumes. Fiber is categorized into two types: soluble and insoluble. Soluble fiber dissolves in water to form a gel-like substance, which can help lower blood cholesterol and glucose levels. Insoluble fiber, on the other hand, adds bulk to the stool and aids in digestion, preventing constipation. Both types of fiber are beneficial for individuals with diabetes, as they can help regulate blood sugar levels and improve overall digestive health.

Research has shown that a high-fiber diet can significantly improve glycemic control in individuals with diabetes. A study published in the New England Journal of Medicine found that participants who consumed a high-fiber diet experienced a 10% reduction in fasting blood glucose levels and a 12% decrease in hemoglobin A1c, a marker of long-term blood sugar control. These findings underscore the importance of incorporating fiber-rich foods into a diabetic diet.

For Sarah, meal planning and preparation can be a daunting task, especially with her busy schedule. However, by focusing on high-fiber, low-glycemic index (GI) foods, she can create nutritious and satisfying meals that support her diabetes management goals. The glycemic index is a ranking system that measures how quickly a carbohydrate-containing food raises blood sugar levels. Foods with a low GI are digested and absorbed more slowly, resulting in a gradual rise in blood sugar levels. Examples of low-GI foods include whole grains like oats and barley, legumes such as lentils and chickpeas, and non-starchy vegetables like broccoli and spinach.

Incorporating these foods into her diet can help Sarah maintain stable blood sugar levels throughout the day. For breakfast, she might enjoy a bowl of oatmeal topped with chia seeds and fresh berries. Oats are a great source of soluble fiber, which can help slow the absorption of glucose and prevent blood sugar spikes. Chia seeds are also rich in fiber and omega-3 fatty acids, which have been shown to improve insulin sensitivity and reduce inflammation. For lunch, a quinoa and black bean salad can provide a satisfying and nutrient-dense meal. Quinoa is a whole grain with a low GI, and black beans are packed with both soluble and insoluble fiber, making this combination an excellent choice for blood sugar control.

When it comes to dinner, Sarah can prepare a lentil and vegetable stew. Lentils are a powerhouse of nutrition, offering a high amount of protein and fiber while being low in fat. They have a low GI and can help stabilize blood sugar levels. By adding a variety of colorful vegetables like carrots, bell peppers, and tomatoes, Sarah can boost the fiber content of the meal and enjoy a delicious, diabetes-friendly dinner.

In addition to choosing the right types of carbohydrates, it is important for Sarah to pay attention to portion sizes. Even healthy, high-fiber foods can cause blood sugar levels to rise if consumed in large quantities. Using measuring cups and food scales can help her keep track of portion sizes and ensure she is not overeating. It is also beneficial for Sarah to spread her carbohydrate intake evenly throughout the day, rather than consuming large amounts in one sitting. This can help prevent blood sugar spikes and crashes, providing her with sustained energy and better glycemic control.

Another practical tip for Sarah is to read food labels carefully. Many packaged foods contain hidden sugars and refined carbohydrates that can negatively impact blood sugar levels. By checking the ingredient list and nutrition facts panel, she can make informed choices and select products that align with her dietary goals. Look for foods that are high in fiber and low in added sugars, and be cautious of terms like "high fructose corn syrup," "cane sugar," and "maltodextrin," which indicate the presence of simple sugars.

Incorporating a variety of high-fiber, low-GI foods into her diet can also help Sarah manage her weight, which is an important aspect of diabetes management. Fiber-rich foods tend to be more filling and can help reduce overall calorie intake by promoting satiety. This can be particularly beneficial for Sarah, who may struggle with weight management due to her busy lifestyle and the demands of her job and family.

For snacks, Sarah can opt for fiber-rich options like raw vegetables with hummus, a handful of nuts, or a piece of fruit with a small serving of Greek yogurt. These snacks are not only nutritious but also convenient and easy to prepare, making them ideal for her on-the-go lifestyle. By keeping healthy snacks on hand, Sarah can avoid the temptation of reaching for sugary or processed foods that can cause blood sugar spikes.

In conclusion, understanding the role of carbohydrates and dietary fiber in a diabetic diet is crucial for effective diabetes management. By prioritizing complex carbohydrates and high-fiber foods, Sarah can maintain stable blood sugar levels, improve her overall health, and enjoy a variety of delicious and satisfying meals. With careful planning and mindful eating, she can navigate the complexities of diabetic nutrition and achieve her health goals.

2.2 Proteins: building a balanced diet

Proteins play a crucial role in managing diabetes, serving as the building blocks of our body and providing essential nutrients that help maintain muscle mass, support metabolic functions, and promote satiety. For individuals like Sarah, who is navigating the complexities of a diabetic diet, understanding the importance of protein and how to incorporate it effectively into meals is vital. Proteins are composed of amino acids, which are necessary for the repair and growth of tissues. Unlike carbohydrates, proteins have a minimal impact on blood sugar levels, making them a critical component of a diabetic-friendly diet. However, not all proteins are created equal, and choosing the right sources is essential for managing diabetes effectively.

Lean proteins are particularly beneficial for those with diabetes as they provide the necessary nutrients without the added fats that can contribute to weight gain and cardiovascular issues. Some of the best sources of lean protein include poultry, fish, legumes, tofu, and low-fat dairy products. For instance, skinless chicken breast is an excellent option as it is low in fat and high in protein. Similarly, fish such as salmon, mackerel, and sardines are rich in omega-3 fatty acids, which have been shown to reduce inflammation and improve heart health, a crucial consideration for diabetics who are at a higher risk of cardiovascular diseases.

Incorporating plant-based proteins like beans, lentils, and tofu can also be beneficial. These sources not only provide protein but also come with the added benefits of fiber, which helps in regulating blood sugar levels. For example, a cup of cooked lentils provides about 18 grams of protein and 15 grams of fiber, making it an excellent choice for a diabetic diet. Additionally, tofu, made from soybeans, is a versatile protein source that can be used in a variety of dishes, from stir-fries to smoothies, offering approximately 10 grams of protein per half-cup serving.

Portion control is another critical aspect of incorporating protein into a diabetic diet. While protein is essential, consuming it in excessive amounts can lead to an increase in calorie intake, which may contribute to weight gain. For Sarah, who is balancing her busy schedule as a teacher and a mother, understanding portion sizes can help her manage her diet more effectively. A general guideline is to aim for about 20-30 grams of protein per meal, which can be achieved through a combination of different protein sources. For example, a meal consisting of a 3-ounce serving of grilled chicken breast (approximately 26 grams of protein), a side of steamed broccoli (about 3 grams of protein), and a small serving of quinoa (about 8 grams of protein per cup) provides a balanced and nutritious meal.

Research has shown that spreading protein intake throughout the day, rather than consuming it all in one meal, can be more beneficial for maintaining muscle mass and managing blood sugar levels. This approach, known as protein pacing, involves consuming moderate amounts of protein at regular intervals, which can help in stabilizing blood sugar levels and preventing spikes. For Sarah, this means incorporating protein-rich snacks between meals, such as a handful of almonds (about 6 grams of protein per ounce) or a small Greek yogurt (approximately 10 grams of protein per serving).

In addition to choosing the right protein sources and managing portion sizes, it is also important to consider the preparation methods. Cooking techniques that minimize the use of added fats and sugars are preferable. For instance, grilling, baking, steaming, and poaching are healthier options compared to frying or sautéing in excessive oil. For example, baking a piece of salmon with a sprinkle of herbs and a squeeze of lemon juice not only enhances the flavor but also keeps the dish low in unhealthy fats.

Case studies have highlighted the positive impact of a balanced protein intake on diabetes management. One study published in the American Journal of Clinical Nutrition found that participants with type 2 diabetes who followed a high-protein diet experienced significant improvements in glycemic control and insulin sensitivity compared to those on a standard protein diet. This underscores the importance of protein in a diabetic diet and its role in improving overall health outcomes.

For Sarah, meal planning can be a daunting task, especially with her busy lifestyle. However, by incorporating a variety of lean protein sources and being mindful of portion sizes, she can create meals that are both nutritious and satisfying. For instance, a weekly meal plan might include a breakfast of scrambled eggs with spinach and tomatoes (about 12 grams of protein), a lunch of grilled chicken salad with mixed greens and a light vinaigrette (about 30 grams of protein), and a dinner of baked cod with a side of roasted vegetables (about 20 grams of protein). Snacks such as a small serving of cottage cheese with fresh berries (about 14 grams of protein) can help keep her energy levels stable throughout the day.

In conclusion, proteins are an indispensable part of a diabetic diet, offering numerous benefits for blood sugar management, muscle maintenance, and overall health. By choosing lean protein sources, managing portion sizes, and opting for healthy cooking methods, individuals like Sarah can effectively incorporate protein into their meals, making their dietary journey more manageable and enjoyable. With the right knowledge and tools, Sarah can feel empowered in her food choices, improve her quality of life, and set a positive example for her family, ensuring that everyone benefits from healthier eating habits.

2.3 Fats and oils: choosing the right types

Fats and oils play a crucial role in our diet, especially for individuals managing diabetes. Understanding the different types of fats and their effects on health can significantly impact blood sugar levels, cardiovascular health, and overall well-being. This subchapter will delve into the various types of fats, highlighting which ones to choose and which to limit, and provide practical tips on incorporating healthy fats into your cooking.

Fats are an essential macronutrient, providing energy, supporting cell growth, protecting organs, and keeping the body warm. They also help in the absorption of certain vitamins and minerals. However, not all fats are created equal. The types of fats you consume can either benefit or harm your health, particularly if you have diabetes. The primary types of fats include saturated fats, trans fats, monounsaturated fats, and polyunsaturated fats.

Saturated fats are typically solid at room temperature and are found in animal products such as meat, butter, cheese, and other full-fat dairy products. They are also present in some plant-based oils like coconut oil and palm oil. Consuming high amounts of saturated fats can raise LDL (low-density lipoprotein) cholesterol levels in the blood, which increases the risk of heart disease. For individuals with diabetes, managing cholesterol levels is crucial since they are already at a higher risk of cardiovascular complications. Therefore, it is advisable to limit the intake of saturated fats.

Trans fats are another type of fat that should be avoided as much as possible. These fats are created through an industrial process that adds hydrogen to liquid vegetable oils to make them more solid. Trans fats are commonly found in processed foods, such as baked goods, snacks, margarine, and fried foods. They not only raise LDL cholesterol levels but also lower HDL (high-density lipoprotein) cholesterol levels, which is the "good" cholesterol. This double impact significantly increases the risk of heart disease and stroke. For people with diabetes, avoiding trans fats is essential for maintaining heart health.

On the other hand, monounsaturated and polyunsaturated fats are considered healthy fats and can be beneficial when included in a balanced diet. Monounsaturated fats are found in foods like avocados, nuts, seeds, and olive oil. These fats can help reduce LDL cholesterol levels and lower the risk of heart disease. They also provide essential nutrients that help develop and maintain the body's cells. Incorporating monounsaturated fats into your diet can be as simple as drizzling olive oil on your salad, adding avocado slices to your sandwich, or snacking on a handful of almonds.

Polyunsaturated fats include omega-3 and omega-6 fatty acids, which are essential fats that the body cannot produce on its own. Omega-3 fatty acids are particularly beneficial for heart health. They can be found in fatty fish such as salmon, mackerel, sardines, and trout, as well as in flaxseeds, chia seeds, and walnuts. Omega-6 fatty acids are found in vegetable oils like soybean oil, corn oil, and sunflower oil. While both types of polyunsaturated fats are important, it is crucial to maintain a balance between omega-3 and omega-6 fatty acids. A diet too high in omega-6 and too low in omega-3 can lead to inflammation and other health issues. For individuals with diabetes, incorporating omega-3 fatty acids can help reduce inflammation and improve heart health.

When it comes to cooking, choosing the right types of fats and oils can make a significant difference. Olive oil, particularly extra-virgin olive oil, is an excellent choice for cooking and salad dressings. It is rich in monounsaturated fats and has been shown to have numerous health benefits, including reducing inflammation and lowering the risk of heart disease. Canola oil is another good option, as it contains both monounsaturated and polyunsaturated fats and has a high smoke point, making it suitable for various cooking methods.

Avocado oil is gaining popularity due to its high content of monounsaturated fats and its versatility in cooking. It has a high smoke point, making it ideal for frying, grilling, and baking. Additionally, it has a mild flavor, which makes it a great addition to salads and marinades. Nut oils, such as walnut oil and almond oil, are also healthy options, but they are best used in dressings or drizzled over dishes rather than for cooking due to their lower smoke points.

Coconut oil, while popular in many health circles, should be used in moderation by individuals with diabetes. Although it is a plant-based oil, it is high in saturated fats, which can raise LDL cholesterol levels. If you choose to use coconut oil, it is best to do so sparingly and in combination with other healthier fats.

Butter and margarine are common fats used in cooking and baking, but they should be consumed with caution. Butter is high in saturated fats, while margarine can contain trans fats, depending on the brand and type. When choosing a spread, look for options that are free of trans fats and lower in saturated fats. Some margarine brands are made with healthier oils and can be a better choice for those managing diabetes.

Incorporating healthy fats into your diet can be done in various ways. Start by replacing unhealthy fats with healthier options. For example, use olive oil instead of butter for sautéing vegetables, or spread avocado on your toast instead of margarine. Snack on nuts and seeds instead of processed snacks, and choose fatty fish like salmon for your protein source a few times a week. These small changes can have a significant impact on your overall health and help manage diabetes more effectively.

Research supports the benefits of healthy fats for individuals with diabetes. A study published in the American Journal of Clinical Nutrition found that a diet rich in monounsaturated fats improved blood sugar control and lipid levels in individuals with type 2 diabetes. Another study in the journal Diabetes Care showed that omega-3 fatty acids from fish oil supplements improved insulin sensitivity and reduced inflammation in people with type 2 diabetes.

Case studies also highlight the positive effects of healthy fats on diabetes management. For instance, Sarah, a 45-year-old high school teacher diagnosed with type 2 diabetes, made significant dietary changes by incorporating more monounsaturated and polyunsaturated fats into her meals. She replaced butter with olive oil, added avocados to her salads, and included fatty fish in her weekly meal plan. Over time, Sarah noticed improvements in her blood sugar levels, cholesterol levels, and overall energy. Her commitment to choosing the right types of fats played a crucial role in her diabetes management journey.

In conclusion, understanding the different types of fats and their effects on health is essential for individuals managing diabetes. By choosing healthy fats like monounsaturated and polyunsaturated fats and limiting saturated and trans fats, you can improve your heart health, manage blood sugar levels, and enhance overall well-being. Incorporating these fats into your cooking and meal planning can be simple and enjoyable, leading to a healthier and more balanced diet. Remember, small changes can make a big difference, and making informed choices about fats and oils is a significant step towards better diabetes management.

SCAN THE QR CODE
TO ACCESS
YOUR EXCLUSIVE BONUS
info@retoteufel.com

3. Breakfasts to start your day

3.1 Oatmeal with chia and berries

Preparation Time: 5 min | Cooking Time: 5 min | Servings: 2

Ingredients:
- Rolled oats: 1/2 cup
- Chia seeds: 2 tablespoons
- Almond milk (unsweetened): 1 cup
- Fresh berries (blueberries, strawberries, raspberries): 1 cup
- Honey (optional): 1 teaspoon
- Vanilla extract: 1/2 teaspoon
- Cinnamon: 1/4 teaspoon

Instructions:
Step 1: In a medium saucepan, combine the rolled oats, chia seeds, and almond milk.
Step 2: Heat the mixture over medium heat, stirring occasionally, for about 5 minutes or until the oats are tender and the mixture thickens.
Step 3: Remove from heat and stir in the vanilla extract and cinnamon.
Step 4: Divide the oatmeal into two bowls.
Step 5: Top each bowl with fresh berries and drizzle with honey if desired.

This oatmeal with chia and berries is a quick and nutritious breakfast option, perfect for those looking to start their day with a balanced, diabetic-friendly meal. The combination of fiber-rich oats and chia seeds with antioxidant-packed berries makes it both delicious and healthy.

Nutritional Values: Calories 220 | Carb 35 g | Protein 6 g | Fiber 9 g | Fat 6 g | Sugar 10 g

3.2 Spinach and feta egg muffins

Preparation Time: 10 min | Cooking Time: 20 min | Servings: 2

Ingredients:
- Eggs: 4 large
- Fresh spinach: 1 cup, chopped
- Feta cheese: 1/2 cup, crumbled
- Red bell pepper: 1/4 cup, finely diced
- Onion: 1/4 cup, finely diced
- Milk: 1/4 cup
- Olive oil: 1 tsp
- Salt: 1/4 tsp
- Black pepper: 1/4 tsp

Instructions:
Step 1: Preheat your oven to 375°F (190°C). Lightly grease a muffin tin with olive oil or use silicone muffin cups.
Step 2: In a medium skillet, heat the olive oil over medium heat. Add the chopped onion and red bell pepper, sautéing until they are soft, about 3-4 minutes.
Step 3: Add the chopped spinach to the skillet and cook until wilted, about 2 minutes. Remove from heat and let cool slightly.
Step 4: In a large bowl, whisk together the eggs, milk, salt, and black pepper.
Step 5: Stir in the sautéed vegetables and crumbled feta cheese.
Step 6: Pour the egg mixture evenly into the prepared muffin tin, filling each cup about 3/4 full.
Step 7: Bake in the preheated oven for 18-20 minutes, or until the egg muffins are set and lightly golden on top.
Step 8: Allow the muffins to cool for a few minutes before removing them from the tin. Serve warm.

These spinach and feta egg muffins are a perfect, protein-packed breakfast option that is both delicious and diabetic-friendly. They are easy to prepare and can be made ahead of time for a quick, nutritious start to your day.

Nutritional Values: Calories 180 | Carbs 3 g | Protein 12 g | Fiber 1 g | Fat 13 g | Sugar 2 g

3.3 Almond butter smoothie

Preparation Time: 5 min | Cooking Time: 0 min | Servings: 2

Ingredients:
- Unsweetened almond milk: 1 cup
- Almond butter: 2 tablespoons
- Frozen banana: 1 large
- Baby spinach: 1 cup
- Chia seeds: 1 tablespoon
- Vanilla extract: 1/2 teaspoon
- Ice cubes: 1 cup

Instructions:
Step 1: Add the unsweetened almond milk, almond butter, frozen banana, baby spinach, chia seeds, vanilla extract, and ice cubes to a high-speed blender.
Step 2: Blend on high until smooth and creamy, scraping down the sides as needed.

Step 3: Pour the smoothie into two glasses and serve immediately.

This almond butter smoothie is a quick and delicious way to start your day. Packed with protein, healthy fats, and low glycemic index fruits, it's perfect for a diabetic-friendly breakfast.

Nutritional Values: Calories 220 | Carb 25 g | Protein 6 g | Fiber 7 g | Fat 12 g | Sugar 9 g

3.4 Cottage cheese and peach parfait

Preparation Time: 10 min | Cooking Time: 0 min | Servings: 2

Ingredients:
- Cottage cheese: 1 cup
- Fresh peaches: 2, diced
- Honey: 2 teaspoons
- Vanilla extract: 1/2 teaspoon
- Almonds: 2 tablespoons, sliced
- Granola: 1/4 cup
- Mint leaves: for garnish (optional)

Instructions:
Step 1: In a small bowl, mix the cottage cheese with the honey and vanilla extract until well combined.
Step 2: In two serving glasses or bowls, layer half of the diced peaches at the bottom.
Step 3: Add a layer of the cottage cheese mixture over the peaches.
Step 4: Sprinkle a tablespoon of granola and a few sliced almonds over the cottage cheese.
Step 5: Repeat the layers with the remaining peaches, cottage cheese mixture, granola, and almonds.
Step 6: Garnish with fresh mint leaves if desired.

This cottage cheese and peach parfait is a delightful, protein-rich breakfast option that is both quick to prepare and perfect for a diabetic-friendly diet. The combination of fresh peaches and creamy cottage cheese provides a refreshing start to your day.

Nutritional Values: Calories 220 | Carb 26 g | Protein 14 g | Fiber 3 g | Fat 8 g | Sugar 18 g

3.5 Turkey and avocado wrap

Preparation Time: 10 min | Cooking Time: 10 min | Servings: 2

Ingredients:
- Whole wheat tortillas: 2 large
- Cooked turkey breast: 6 oz, thinly sliced
- Avocado: 1, sliced
- Romaine lettuce: 2 leaves, chopped
- Cherry tomatoes: 6, halved
- Red onion: 1/4, thinly sliced

- Greek yogurt: 2 tbsp
- Lemon juice: 1 tsp
- Salt: to taste
- Black pepper: to taste

Instructions:
Step 1: In a small bowl, mix the Greek yogurt and lemon juice. Season with salt and black pepper to taste.
Step 2: Lay the tortillas flat on a clean surface. Spread the yogurt mixture evenly over each tortilla.
Step 3: Layer the turkey slices, avocado slices, chopped romaine lettuce, cherry tomatoes, and red onion evenly on each tortilla.
Step 4: Roll up each tortilla tightly to form a wrap. Cut each wrap in half diagonally.
Step 5: Serve immediately or wrap in foil for an on-the-go breakfast.

This turkey and avocado wrap is a perfect diabetic-friendly breakfast option. It's quick to prepare, packed with protein, healthy fats, and fiber to keep you full and energized throughout the morning.

Nutritional Values: Calories 320 | Carbs 30 g | Protein 25 g | Fiber 8 g | Fat 15 g | Sugar 3 g

3.6 Quinoa and apple breakfast bowl

Preparation Time: 10 min | Cooking Time: 10 min | Servings: 2

Ingredients:
- Quinoa: 1/2 cup
- Water: 1 cup
- Apple: 1 medium, diced
- Almond milk: 1/2 cup
- Cinnamon: 1/2 tsp
- Honey: 1 tbsp
- Chia seeds: 1 tbsp
- Walnuts: 2 tbsp, chopped
- Blueberries: 1/4 cup

Instructions:
Step 1: Rinse the quinoa under cold water.
Step 2: In a medium saucepan, combine the quinoa and water. Bring to a boil, then reduce the heat to low, cover, and simmer for about 10 minutes, or until the water is absorbed and the quinoa is tender.
Step 3: While the quinoa is cooking, dice the apple and set aside.
Step 4: Once the quinoa is cooked, remove from heat and let it sit covered for 5 minutes, then fluff with a fork.
Step 5: In a bowl, combine the cooked quinoa, almond milk, diced apple, cinnamon, and honey. Mix well.
Step 6: Divide the mixture into two bowls. Top each bowl with chia seeds, chopped walnuts, and blueberries.

This quinoa and apple breakfast bowl is a nutritious and delicious way to start your day. It's packed with protein, fiber, and healthy fats, making it perfect for a diabetic-friendly diet.

Nutritional Values: Calories 320 | Carb 50 g | Protein 8 g | Fiber 7 g | Fat 12 g | Sugar 15 g

3.7 Greek yogurt with nuts and honey

Preparation Time: 5 min | Cooking Time: 0 min | Servings: 2

Ingredients:
- Greek yogurt: 1 cup
- Mixed nuts (almonds, walnuts, and pistachios): 1/4 cup
- Honey: 2 tablespoons
- Fresh berries (optional): 1/4 cup

Instructions:
Step 1: Divide the Greek yogurt evenly between two bowls.
Step 2: Roughly chop the mixed nuts and sprinkle them over the yogurt.
Step 3: Drizzle 1 tablespoon of honey over each bowl.
Step 4: Optionally, top with fresh berries for added flavor and nutrients.

This delightful breakfast is not only quick and easy to prepare but also packed with protein and healthy fats, making it a perfect diabetic-friendly option to start your day.

Nutritional Values: Calories 250 | Carbs 25 g | Protein 10 g | Fiber 2 g | Fat 12 g | Sugar 18 g

3.8 Tofu scramble with vegetables

Preparation Time: 10 min | Cooking Time: 10 min | Servings: 2

Ingredients:
- Firm tofu: 8 oz (225 g), drained and crumbled
- Olive oil: 1 tbsp
- Onion: 1/2 small, finely chopped
- Bell pepper: 1/2 medium, diced
- Cherry tomatoes: 1/2 cup, halved
- Spinach: 1 cup, chopped
- Turmeric: 1/2 tsp
- Garlic powder: 1/4 tsp
- Salt: 1/4 tsp
- Black pepper: 1/8 tsp
- Nutritional yeast: 1 tbsp (optional)
- Fresh parsley: 1 tbsp, chopped (for garnish)

Instructions:
Step 1: Heat the olive oil in a large skillet over medium heat.
Step 2: Add the chopped onion and bell pepper, and sauté for 3-4 minutes until softened.
Step 3: Add the cherry tomatoes and cook for another 2 minutes.
Step 4: Stir in the crumbled tofu, turmeric, garlic powder, salt, and black pepper. Cook for 5 minutes, stirring

occasionally.
Step 5: Add the chopped spinach and cook until wilted, about 1-2 minutes.
Step 6: If using, sprinkle the nutritional yeast over the tofu scramble and mix well.
Step 7: Garnish with fresh parsley before serving.

This tofu scramble with vegetables is a quick and nutritious breakfast option, perfect for those following a diabetic-friendly diet. It's packed with protein and fiber to keep you full and energized throughout the morning.

Nutritional Values: Calories 200 | Carb 10 g | Protein 18 g | Fiber 4 g | Fat 12 g | Sugar 3 g

3.9 Buckwheat pancakes

Preparation Time: 10 min | Cooking Time: 10 min | Servings: 2

Ingredients:
- Buckwheat flour: 1/2 cup
- Whole wheat flour: 1/4 cup
- Baking powder: 1 tsp
- Baking soda: 1/4 tsp
- Salt: 1/4 tsp
- Buttermilk: 1 cup
- Egg: 1 large
- Unsweetened applesauce: 2 tbsp
- Vanilla extract: 1/2 tsp
- Olive oil: 1 tbsp
- Fresh berries (optional): 1/2 cup

Instructions:
Step 1: In a large bowl, whisk together the buckwheat flour, whole wheat flour, baking powder, baking soda, and salt.
Step 2: In another bowl, whisk together the buttermilk, egg, applesauce, vanilla extract, and olive oil until well combined.
Step 3: Pour the wet ingredients into the dry ingredients and stir until just combined. Do not overmix.
Step 4: Heat a non-stick skillet or griddle over medium heat and lightly grease with a little olive oil.
Step 5: Pour 1/4 cup of batter onto the skillet for each pancake. Cook until bubbles form on the surface and the edges look set, about 2-3 minutes.
Step 6: Flip the pancakes and cook for another 2-3 minutes, or until golden brown and cooked through.
Step 7: Serve warm with fresh berries if desired.

These buckwheat pancakes are not only delicious but also packed with fiber and protein, making them a perfect diabetic-friendly breakfast option to start your day right.

Nutritional Values: Calories 220 | Carbs 30 g | Protein 8 g | Fiber 5 g | Fat 7 g | Sugar 4 g

3.10 Chia pudding with coconut milk

Preparation Time: 10 min | Cooking Time: 10 min | Servings: 2

Ingredients:
- Chia seeds: 1/4 cup
- Coconut milk: 1 cup (full-fat or light)
- Vanilla extract: 1/2 teaspoon
- Maple syrup: 1 tablespoon (optional)
- Fresh berries: 1/2 cup (for topping)
- Unsweetened shredded coconut: 2 tablespoons (for topping)

Instructions:
Step 1: In a medium bowl, combine chia seeds, coconut milk, vanilla extract, and maple syrup (if using).
Step 2: Stir well to ensure the chia seeds are evenly distributed in the coconut milk.
Step 3: Cover the bowl and refrigerate for at least 4 hours or overnight to allow the chia seeds to absorb the liquid and form a pudding-like consistency.
Step 4: Before serving, give the chia pudding a good stir to break up any clumps.
Step 5: Divide the chia pudding into two serving bowls.
Step 6: Top each serving with fresh berries and a sprinkle of unsweetened shredded coconut.

Chia pudding with coconut milk is a delicious and nutritious breakfast option, perfect for a diabetic-friendly diet. It's rich in fiber, healthy fats, and low in sugar, making it a balanced start to your day.

Nutritional Values: Calories 200 | Carbs 14 g | Protein 4 g | Fiber 8 g | Fat 14 g | Sugar 4 g

3.11 Smoked salmon and cream cheese bagel

Preparation Time: 10 min | Cooking Time: 10 min | Servings: 2

Ingredients:
- Whole wheat bagels: 2
- Smoked salmon: 4 oz
- Cream cheese (low-fat): 4 tbsp
- Red onion: 1/4, thinly sliced
- Capers: 2 tsp
- Fresh dill: 2 sprigs, chopped
- Lemon: 1, cut into wedges
- Black pepper: to taste

Instructions:
Step 1: Slice the whole wheat bagels in half and toast them until they are golden brown.
Step 2: Spread 2 tablespoons of low-fat cream cheese on each bagel half.
Step 3: Layer 1 oz of smoked salmon on top of the cream cheese on each bagel half.
Step 4: Add a few slices of red onion and a sprinkle of capers on top of the smoked salmon.
Step 5: Garnish with fresh dill and a squeeze of lemon juice.

Step 6: Season with black pepper to taste and serve immediately.

This smoked salmon and cream cheese bagel is a quick and delicious breakfast option that is both nutritious and diabetic-friendly. The combination of whole grains, lean protein, and healthy fats provides a balanced start to your day.

Nutritional Values: Calories 320 | Carbs 42 g | Protein 18 g | Fiber 5 g | Fat 10 g | Sugar 5 g

3.12 Kale and sweet potato hash

Preparation Time: 10 min | Cooking Time: 20 min | Servings: 2

Ingredients:
- Sweet potatoes: 2 medium (about 1 lb), peeled and diced
- Kale: 2 cups, chopped
- Olive oil: 2 tablespoons
- Onion: 1 small, diced
- Red bell pepper: 1/2, diced
- Garlic: 2 cloves, minced
- Ground cumin: 1 teaspoon
- Paprika: 1/2 teaspoon
- Salt: 1/2 teaspoon
- Black pepper: 1/4 teaspoon
- Eggs: 2 large

Instructions:
Step 1: Heat 1 tablespoon of olive oil in a large skillet over medium heat. Add the diced sweet potatoes and cook for about 10 minutes, stirring occasionally, until they start to soften.
Step 2: Add the remaining 1 tablespoon of olive oil to the skillet, then add the diced onion, red bell pepper, and minced garlic. Cook for another 5 minutes until the vegetables are tender.
Step 3: Stir in the chopped kale, ground cumin, paprika, salt, and black pepper. Cook for an additional 5 minutes, stirring occasionally, until the kale is wilted and the sweet potatoes are fully cooked.
Step 4: In a separate non-stick skillet, cook the eggs to your preference (sunny-side up, over-easy, or scrambled).
Step 5: Divide the sweet potato and kale hash between two plates and top each with a cooked egg.

This kale and sweet potato hash is a nutrient-dense, diabetic-friendly breakfast option that is quick and easy to prepare. It's packed with fiber, vitamins, and protein to help you start your day right.

Nutritional Values: Calories 300 | Carb 45 g | Protein 10 g | Fiber 8 g | Fat 12 g | Sugar 8 g

3.13 Blueberry and almond oat bars

Preparation Time: 10 min | Cooking Time: 25 min | Servings: 2

Ingredients:
- Rolled oats: 1 cup
- Almond flour: 1/2 cup
- Blueberries: 1/2 cup
- Almond butter: 1/4 cup
- Honey: 2 tbsp
- Vanilla extract: 1 tsp
- Cinnamon: 1/2 tsp
- Salt: 1/4 tsp
- Baking powder: 1/2 tsp
- Egg: 1 large

Instructions:
Step 1: Preheat your oven to 350°F (175°C) and line an 8x8 inch baking pan with parchment paper.
Step 2: In a large bowl, mix together the rolled oats, almond flour, cinnamon, salt, and baking powder.
Step 3: In a separate bowl, whisk together the almond butter, honey, vanilla extract, and egg until smooth.
Step 4: Pour the wet ingredients into the dry ingredients and mix until well combined.
Step 5: Gently fold in the blueberries.
Step 6: Spread the mixture evenly into the prepared baking pan.
Step 7: Bake for 20-25 minutes, or until the edges are golden brown and a toothpick inserted into the center comes out clean.
Step 8: Allow the bars to cool completely in the pan before cutting into squares.

These blueberry and almond oat bars are a perfect diabetic-friendly breakfast option. They are high in fiber, low in sugar, and packed with nutritious ingredients to start your day right.

Nutritional Values: Calories 220 | Carb 28 g | Protein 7 g | Fiber 5 g | Fat 10 g | Sugar 10 g

3.14 Ricotta and pear toast

Preparation Time: 10 min | Cooking Time: 10 min | Servings: 2

Ingredients:
- Whole grain bread: 4 slices
- Ricotta cheese: 1/2 cup
- Pear: 1, thinly sliced
- Honey: 2 teaspoons
- Ground cinnamon: 1/2 teaspoon
- Chopped walnuts: 2 tablespoons
- Lemon juice: 1 teaspoon

Instructions:
Step 1: Toast the whole grain bread slices until they are golden brown and crispy.
Step 2: While the bread is toasting, mix the ricotta cheese with the lemon juice in a small bowl until smooth.
Step 3: Spread the ricotta mixture evenly over the toasted bread slices.
Step 4: Arrange the thinly sliced pear on top of the ricotta cheese.

Step 5: Drizzle honey over the pear slices.
Step 6: Sprinkle ground cinnamon and chopped walnuts on top for added flavor and crunch.

This ricotta and pear toast is a delightful and nutritious breakfast option. The combination of creamy ricotta, sweet pear, and crunchy walnuts provides a balanced meal that is both satisfying and diabetic-friendly.

Nutritional Values: Calories 220 | Carbs 28 g | Protein 9 g | Fiber 4 g | Fat 9 g | Sugar 12 g

3.15 Vegetable omelette

Preparation Time: 10 min | Cooking Time: 10 min | Servings: 2

Ingredients:
- Eggs: 4 large
- Bell pepper: 1/2 cup, diced
- Onion: 1/4 cup, finely chopped
- Spinach: 1 cup, fresh
- Cherry tomatoes: 1/2 cup, halved
- Olive oil: 1 tablespoon
- Salt: 1/4 teaspoon
- Black pepper: 1/4 teaspoon
- Low-fat cheese: 1/4 cup, shredded

Instructions:
Step 1: In a medium bowl, whisk the eggs until well combined. Season with salt and black pepper.
Step 2: Heat olive oil in a non-stick skillet over medium heat. Add the diced bell pepper and chopped onion. Sauté for 3-4 minutes until softened.
Step 3: Add the spinach and cherry tomatoes to the skillet. Cook for another 2 minutes until the spinach is wilted.
Step 4: Pour the whisked eggs over the vegetables in the skillet. Allow the eggs to set around the edges.
Step 5: Sprinkle the shredded low-fat cheese evenly over the omelette. Cook for 2-3 minutes until the eggs are fully set and the cheese is melted.
Step 6: Carefully fold the omelette in half and slide it onto a plate. Serve hot.

This vegetable omelette is a quick and nutritious way to start your day, packed with protein and fiber to keep you energized and satisfied.

Nutritional Values: Calories 250 | Carbs 8 g | Protein 18 g | Fiber 3 g | Fat 16 g | Sugar 4 g

3.16 Protein-packed breakfast tacos

Preparation Time: 10 min | Cooking Time: 10 min | Servings: 2

Ingredients:
- Eggs: 4 large

- Black beans: 1/2 cup, drained and rinsed
- Cherry tomatoes: 1/2 cup, halved
- Red onion: 1/4 cup, finely chopped
- Avocado: 1 small, diced
- Fresh cilantro: 2 tablespoons, chopped
- Lime: 1, juiced
- Olive oil: 1 tablespoon
- Whole wheat tortillas: 4 small
- Salt: to taste
- Black pepper: to taste

Instructions:
Step 1: In a medium bowl, whisk the eggs with a pinch of salt and black pepper.
Step 2: Heat the olive oil in a non-stick skillet over medium heat. Add the eggs and scramble until fully cooked. Set aside.
Step 3: In a separate bowl, combine the black beans, cherry tomatoes, red onion, avocado, cilantro, and lime juice. Mix well.
Step 4: Warm the tortillas in a dry skillet over medium heat for about 30 seconds on each side.
Step 5: Divide the scrambled eggs evenly among the tortillas.
Step 6: Top each tortilla with the black bean and avocado mixture.
Step 7: Serve immediately, garnished with extra cilantro if desired.

These protein-packed breakfast tacos are not only delicious but also provide a balanced start to your day with a good mix of protein, fiber, and healthy fats. Perfect for a diabetic-friendly diet!

Nutritional Values: Calories 350 | Carb 35 g | Protein 20 g | Fiber 10 g | Fat 15 g | Sugar 3 g

3.17 Banana and walnut bread

Preparation Time: 15 min | Cooking Time: 50 min | Servings: 2

Ingredients:
- All-purpose flour: 1 cup
- Baking soda: 1/2 teaspoon
- Salt: 1/4 teaspoon
- Unsalted butter: 1/4 cup (softened)
- Brown sugar: 1/4 cup
- Egg: 1 large
- Ripe bananas: 2 medium (mashed)
- Vanilla extract: 1/2 teaspoon
- Plain Greek yogurt: 1/4 cup
- Chopped walnuts: 1/4 cup

Instructions:
Step 1: Preheat your oven to 350°F (175°C). Grease a 9x5 inch loaf pan or line it with parchment paper.
Step 2: In a medium bowl, whisk together the flour, baking soda, and salt.

Step 3: In a separate large bowl, cream the butter and brown sugar until light and fluffy. Beat in the egg, then stir in the mashed bananas and vanilla extract.
Step 4: Add the flour mixture to the banana mixture and stir until just combined. Fold in the Greek yogurt and chopped walnuts.
Step 5: Pour the batter into the prepared loaf pan and smooth the top.
Step 6: Bake in the preheated oven for 50 minutes, or until a toothpick inserted into the center comes out clean.
Step 7: Allow the bread to cool in the pan for 10 minutes, then transfer to a wire rack to cool completely before slicing.

This banana and walnut bread is not only delicious but also packed with nutrients. The bananas provide natural sweetness and fiber, while the walnuts add a satisfying crunch and healthy fats. Perfect for a diabetic-friendly breakfast!

Nutritional Values: Calories 280 | Carbs 38 g | Protein 6 g | Fiber 3 g | Fat 12 g | Sugar 14 g

3.18 Green detox smoothie

Preparation Time: 10 min | Cooking Time: 0 min | Servings: 2

Ingredients:
- Spinach: 2 cups
- Kale: 1 cup
- Green apple: 1, cored and chopped
- Banana: 1, frozen
- Avocado: 1/2, peeled and pitted
- Chia seeds: 1 tablespoon
- Almond milk: 1 cup, unsweetened
- Ice cubes: 1/2 cup

Instructions:
Step 1: Add spinach, kale, green apple, banana, avocado, chia seeds, and almond milk to a blender.
Step 2: Blend on high until smooth and creamy.
Step 3: Add ice cubes and blend again until the desired consistency is reached.
Step 4: Pour into two glasses and serve immediately.

This green detox smoothie is packed with nutrients and fiber, making it an excellent choice for a diabetic-friendly breakfast. It's quick to prepare and provides a refreshing, energizing start to your day.

Nutritional Values: Calories 200 | Carb 30 g | Protein 5 g | Fiber 8 g | Fat 9 g | Sugar 14 g

4. Nutritious and satisfying lunches
4.1 Turkey and avocado wrap

Preparation Time: 10 min | Cooking Time: 10 min | Servings: 2

Ingredients:
- Whole wheat tortillas: 2 large
- Cooked turkey breast: 6 oz, thinly sliced
- Avocado: 1, sliced
- Romaine lettuce: 4 leaves, chopped
- Tomato: 1 medium, diced
- Red onion: 1/4 small, thinly sliced
- Greek yogurt: 2 tbsp
- Dijon mustard: 1 tsp
- Lemon juice: 1 tsp
- Salt: to taste
- Black pepper: to taste

Instructions:
Step 1: In a small bowl, mix the Greek yogurt, Dijon mustard, lemon juice, salt, and black pepper to make the dressing.
Step 2: Lay out the tortillas on a flat surface. Spread an even layer of the dressing on each tortilla.
Step 3: Place the chopped romaine lettuce in the center of each tortilla.
Step 4: Layer the turkey slices, avocado slices, diced tomato, and thinly sliced red onion on top of the lettuce.
Step 5: Fold in the sides of the tortilla and then roll it up tightly from the bottom to form a wrap.
Step 6: Cut each wrap in half diagonally and serve immediately.

This turkey and avocado wrap is a perfect blend of lean protein, healthy fats, and fresh vegetables, making it a nutritious and satisfying lunch option that supports blood sugar management.

Nutritional Values: Calories 350 | Carbs 35 g | Protein 25 g | Fiber 8 g | Fat 15 g | Sugar 5 g

4.2 Quinoa and black bean salad

Preparation Time: 10 min | Cooking Time: 10 min | Servings: 2

Ingredients:
- Quinoa: 1/2 cup (uncooked)
- Black beans: 1 cup (cooked, drained, and rinsed)
- Red bell pepper: 1/2 cup (diced)
- Corn kernels: 1/2 cup (cooked)
- Red onion: 1/4 cup (finely chopped)
- Cilantro: 1/4 cup (chopped)
- Lime juice: 2 tablespoons
- Olive oil: 1 tablespoon
- Cumin: 1/2 teaspoon
- Salt: 1/4 teaspoon
- Black pepper: 1/4 teaspoon

Instructions:
Step 1: Cook the quinoa according to the package instructions. Once cooked, let it cool to room temperature.
Step 2: In a large bowl, combine the cooked quinoa, black beans, red bell pepper, corn kernels, red onion, and cilantro.
Step 3: In a small bowl, whisk together the lime juice, olive oil, cumin, salt, and black pepper.
Step 4: Pour the dressing over the quinoa mixture and toss to combine.
Step 5: Serve immediately or refrigerate for up to 2 days.

This quinoa and black bean salad is a perfect blend of flavors and textures, providing a nutritious and satisfying lunch option that supports blood sugar management. It's quick to prepare and packed with protein and fiber.

Nutritional Values: Calories 320 | Carb 50 g | Protein 10 g | Fiber 12 g | Fat 9 g | Sugar 4 g

4.3 Grilled chicken caesar salad

Preparation Time: 15 min | Cooking Time: 10 min | Servings: 2

Ingredients:
- Chicken breast: 2 (about 6 oz each)
- Olive oil: 2 tbsp
- Romaine lettuce: 1 large head, chopped
- Parmesan cheese: 1/4 cup, grated
- Caesar dressing: 1/4 cup
- Croutons: 1/2 cup
- Lemon: 1, cut into wedges
- Salt: to taste
- Black pepper: to taste

Instructions:

Step 1: Preheat the grill to medium-high heat. Brush the chicken breasts with olive oil and season with salt and black pepper.
Step 2: Grill the chicken breasts for about 5-7 minutes on each side, or until fully cooked and the internal temperature reaches 165°F. Remove from the grill and let rest for a few minutes before slicing.
Step 3: In a large bowl, combine the chopped romaine lettuce, grated Parmesan cheese, and croutons.
Step 4: Add the Caesar dressing to the bowl and toss the salad until all ingredients are evenly coated.
Step 5: Slice the grilled chicken breasts into thin strips and place on top of the salad.
Step 6: Serve the salad with lemon wedges on the side for an extra burst of freshness.

This Grilled Chicken Caesar Salad is a perfect blend of flavors and textures, offering a nutritious and satisfying lunch option that supports blood sugar management. It's quick to prepare and packed with protein to keep you energized throughout the day.

Nutritional Values: Calories 450 | Carb 20 g | Protein 35 g | Fiber 5 g | Fat 25 g | Sugar 3 g

4.4 Vegetable lentil soup

Preparation Time: 15 min | Cooking Time: 30 min | Servings: 2

Ingredients:
- Olive oil: 1 tablespoon
- Yellow onion, diced: 1 small
- Carrots, diced: 2 medium
- Celery stalks, diced: 2
- Garlic cloves, minced: 2
- Ground cumin: 1 teaspoon
- Ground coriander: 1 teaspoon
- Ground turmeric: 1/2 teaspoon
- Red lentils, rinsed: 1/2 cup
- Diced tomatoes: 1 can (14.5 ounces)
- Vegetable broth: 4 cups
- Baby spinach: 2 cups
- Lemon juice: 1 tablespoon
- Salt: to taste
- Black pepper: to taste

Instructions:

Step 1: Heat the olive oil in a large pot over medium heat. Add the diced onion, carrots, and celery. Sauté for about 5 minutes, until the vegetables begin to soften.
Step 2: Add the minced garlic, ground cumin, ground coriander, and ground turmeric to the pot. Stir and cook for another 1-2 minutes until fragrant.
Step 3: Add the rinsed red lentils, diced tomatoes (with their juice), and vegetable broth to the pot. Stir to combine.
Step 4: Bring the mixture to a boil, then reduce the heat to low and let it simmer for about 20-25 minutes, or until the lentils and vegetables are tender.

Step 5: Stir in the baby spinach and cook for an additional 2-3 minutes, until the spinach is wilted.
Step 6: Add the lemon juice and season with salt and black pepper to taste. Serve hot.

This vegetable lentil soup is a perfect blend of flavors and nutrients, making it an ideal choice for a wholesome and satisfying lunch. It's quick to prepare and packed with protein and fiber to keep you full and energized throughout the day.

Nutritional Values: Calories 250 | Carbs 40 g | Protein 12 g | Fiber 10 g | Fat 6 g | Sugar 8 g

4.5 Spinach and feta stuffed chicken

Preparation Time: 15 min | Cooking Time: 25 min | Servings: 2

Ingredients:
- Chicken breasts: 2 large
- Fresh spinach: 2 cups, chopped
- Feta cheese: 1/2 cup, crumbled
- Olive oil: 1 tablespoon
- Garlic: 2 cloves, minced
- Lemon zest: 1 teaspoon
- Salt: 1/2 teaspoon
- Black pepper: 1/4 teaspoon
- Toothpicks: as needed

Instructions:
Step 1: Preheat your oven to 375°F (190°C).
Step 2: In a skillet, heat olive oil over medium heat. Add minced garlic and sauté until fragrant, about 1 minute.
Step 3: Add chopped spinach to the skillet and cook until wilted, about 2-3 minutes. Remove from heat and let cool slightly.
Step 4: In a bowl, combine the cooked spinach, crumbled feta cheese, and lemon zest. Mix well.
Step 5: Butterfly the chicken breasts by slicing them horizontally but not all the way through, creating a pocket.
Step 6: Stuff each chicken breast with the spinach and feta mixture. Secure with toothpicks if necessary.
Step 7: Season the stuffed chicken breasts with salt and black pepper.
Step 8: Place the stuffed chicken breasts in a baking dish and bake in the preheated oven for 25 minutes, or until the chicken is cooked through and no longer pink in the center.
Step 9: Remove from the oven and let rest for a few minutes before serving.

This recipe combines the rich flavors of spinach and feta in a diabetes-friendly dish that's both nutritious and satisfying. Simple to prepare, it supports your healthy eating goals without compromising on taste.

Nutritional Values: Calories: 320 | Carbs: 3 g | Sugar: 1 g | Protein: 42 g | Fat: 15 g

4.6 Roasted vegetable and hummus wrap

Preparation Time: 15 min | Cooking Time: 25 min | Servings: 2

Ingredients:
- Whole wheat tortillas: 2 large
- Red bell pepper: 1, sliced
- Zucchini: 1 medium, sliced
- Red onion: 1 small, sliced
- Olive oil: 2 tablespoons
- Salt: 1/2 teaspoon
- Black pepper: 1/4 teaspoon
- Hummus: 1/2 cup
- Baby spinach: 1 cup
- Feta cheese: 1/4 cup, crumbled (optional)

Instructions:
Step 1: Preheat the oven to 425°F (220°C).
Step 2: On a baking sheet, toss the red bell pepper, zucchini, and red onion with olive oil, salt, and black pepper.
Step 3: Roast the vegetables in the preheated oven for 20-25 minutes, or until tender and slightly charred.
Step 4: Warm the tortillas in a dry skillet over medium heat for about 30 seconds on each side.
Step 5: Spread 1/4 cup of hummus evenly over each tortilla.
Step 6: Divide the roasted vegetables evenly between the two tortillas, placing them on top of the hummus.
Step 7: Add 1/2 cup of baby spinach to each wrap and sprinkle with feta cheese if using.
Step 8: Roll up the tortillas tightly, slice in half, and serve immediately.

This roasted vegetable and hummus wrap is a perfect blend of flavors and textures, offering a nutritious and satisfying lunch option that supports blood sugar management. It's quick to prepare and packed with wholesome ingredients.

Nutritional Values: Calories 350 | Carbs 45 g | Protein 10 g | Fiber 8 g | Fat 15 g | Sugar 8 g

4.7 Tuna salad stuffed tomatoes

Preparation Time: 15 min | Cooking Time: 0 min | Servings: 2

Ingredients:
- Large tomatoes: 2
- Canned tuna (in water), drained: 1 can (5 oz)
- Greek yogurt: 1/4 cup
- Celery, finely chopped: 1/4 cup
- Red onion, finely chopped: 2 tbsp
- Fresh parsley, chopped: 1 tbsp
- Lemon juice: 1 tbsp
- Dijon mustard: 1 tsp
- Salt: 1/4 tsp
- Black pepper: 1/4 tsp
- Mixed greens: 2 cups

Instructions:
Step 1: Cut the tops off the tomatoes and scoop out the insides, leaving a hollow shell. Set the tomato shells aside.
Step 2: In a medium bowl, combine the drained tuna, Greek yogurt, celery, red onion, parsley, lemon juice, Dijon mustard, salt, and black pepper. Mix well until all ingredients are thoroughly combined.
Step 3: Stuff each tomato shell with the tuna salad mixture, pressing down gently to fill completely.
Step 4: Serve the stuffed tomatoes on a bed of mixed greens.

This delightful recipe is quick to prepare and packed with protein and healthy fats, making it a perfect nutritious and satisfying lunch option.

Nutritional Values: Calories 180 | Carbs 10 g | Protein 25 g | Fiber 3 g | Fat 5 g | Sugar 6 g

4.8 Broccoli and cheddar stuffed potatoes

Preparation Time: 15 min | Cooking Time: 60 min | Servings: 2

Ingredients:
- Russet potatoes: 2 large
- Broccoli florets: 1 cup
- Cheddar cheese, shredded: 1 cup
- Greek yogurt: 1/4 cup
- Olive oil: 1 tbsp
- Garlic powder: 1/2 tsp
- Salt: 1/2 tsp
- Black pepper: 1/4 tsp
- Green onions, chopped: 2 tbsp

Instructions:
Step 1: Preheat your oven to 400°F (200°C). Wash and scrub the russet potatoes thoroughly.
Step 2: Pierce each potato several times with a fork. Rub them with olive oil and place them on a baking sheet. Bake for 45-50 minutes, or until tender.
Step 3: While the potatoes are baking, steam the broccoli florets until tender, about 5-7 minutes. Set aside.
Step 4: Once the potatoes are done, let them cool slightly. Cut each potato in half lengthwise and scoop out the insides, leaving a small border of potato around the skin.
Step 5: In a bowl, mash the scooped-out potato with Greek yogurt, garlic powder, salt, and black pepper until smooth.
Step 6: Stir in the steamed broccoli and half of the shredded cheddar cheese into the mashed potato mixture.
Step 7: Spoon the mixture back into the potato skins. Top with the remaining cheddar cheese.
Step 8: Return the stuffed potatoes to the oven and bake for an additional 10 minutes, or until the cheese is melted and bubbly.
Step 9: Garnish with chopped green onions before serving.

This hearty recipe brings together the comforting flavors of broccoli and cheddar in a satisfying diabetic-friendly dish. Easy to make, it's a delicious way to enjoy balanced carbs and protein.

Nutritional Values: Calories: 420 | Carbs: 58 g | Sugar: 4 g | Protein: 19 g | Fat: 15 g

4.9 Asian chicken salad

Preparation Time: 15 min | Cooking Time: 10 min | Servings: 2

Ingredients:
- Chicken breast: 1 (about 8 oz)
- Mixed greens: 4 cups
- Red bell pepper: 1, thinly sliced
- Carrot: 1, julienned
- Cucumber: 1/2, thinly sliced
- Green onions: 2, chopped
- Cilantro: 1/4 cup, chopped
- Sesame seeds: 1 tbsp
- Olive oil: 1 tbsp
- Soy sauce: 2 tbsp
- Rice vinegar: 1 tbsp
- Honey: 1 tsp
- Sesame oil: 1 tsp
- Garlic: 1 clove, minced
- Fresh ginger: 1 tsp, grated
- Salt: to taste
- Black pepper: to taste

Instructions:
Step 1: Season the chicken breast with salt and black pepper. Heat olive oil in a skillet over medium heat and cook the chicken breast for about 5-7 minutes on each side, or until fully cooked. Let it rest for a few minutes, then slice thinly.
Step 2: In a large bowl, combine mixed greens, red bell pepper, carrot, cucumber, green onions, and cilantro.
Step 3: In a small bowl, whisk together soy sauce, rice vinegar, honey, sesame oil, garlic, and fresh ginger to make the dressing.
Step 4: Add the sliced chicken to the salad and drizzle with the dressing. Toss to combine.
Step 5: Sprinkle sesame seeds on top before serving.

This Asian Chicken Salad is a perfect blend of flavors and textures, offering a nutritious and satisfying lunch option that supports blood sugar management. It's quick to prepare and packed with fresh, wholesome ingredients.

Nutritional Values: Calories 350 | Carbs 20 g | Protein 30 g | Fiber 5 g | Fat 15 g | Sugar 10 g

4.10 Mediterranean chickpea wrap

Preparation Time: 15 min | Cooking Time: 0 min | Servings: 2

Ingredients:
- Whole wheat tortillas: 2 (8-inch)
- Canned chickpeas: 1 cup, drained and rinsed
- Cherry tomatoes: 1/2 cup, halved
- Cucumber: 1/2 cup, diced
- Red onion: 1/4 cup, finely chopped
- Kalamata olives: 1/4 cup, pitted and sliced
- Feta cheese: 1/4 cup, crumbled
- Fresh parsley: 2 tablespoons, chopped
- Lemon juice: 1 tablespoon
- Extra virgin olive oil: 1 tablespoon
- Garlic: 1 clove, minced
- Salt: 1/4 teaspoon
- Black pepper: 1/4 teaspoon

Instructions:
Step 1: In a medium bowl, combine chickpeas, cherry tomatoes, cucumber, red onion, olives, feta cheese, and parsley.
Step 2: In a small bowl, whisk together lemon juice, olive oil, garlic, salt, and black pepper.
Step 3: Pour the dressing over the chickpea mixture and toss to coat evenly.
Step 4: Warm the tortillas in a dry skillet over medium heat for about 30 seconds on each side.
Step 5: Divide the chickpea mixture evenly between the two tortillas.
Step 6: Roll up the tortillas tightly, tucking in the sides as you go, to form wraps.
Step 7: Slice each wrap in half and serve immediately.

This Mediterranean Chickpea Wrap is a perfect blend of fresh vegetables, protein-rich chickpeas, and tangy feta, making it a nutritious and satisfying lunch option. It's quick to prepare and packed with flavors that will keep you energized throughout the day.

Nutritional Values: Calories 350 | Carbs 45 g | Protein 12 g | Fiber 10 g | Fat 14 g | Sugar 5 g

4.11 Zucchini noodle and shrimp bowl

Preparation Time: 10 min | Cooking Time: 10 min | Servings: 2

Ingredients:
- Zucchini: 2 medium, spiralized
- Shrimp: 12 oz, peeled and deveined
- Olive oil: 2 tbsp
- Garlic: 2 cloves, minced
- Cherry tomatoes: 1 cup, halved
- Red bell pepper: 1, thinly sliced
- Lemon juice: 2 tbsp
- Fresh parsley: 2 tbsp, chopped
- Salt: to taste

- Black pepper: to taste
- Red pepper flakes: 1/4 tsp (optional)

Instructions:
Step 1: Heat 1 tablespoon of olive oil in a large skillet over medium heat. Add the shrimp, season with salt and black pepper, and cook for 2-3 minutes on each side until pink and opaque. Remove from the skillet and set aside.
Step 2: In the same skillet, add the remaining tablespoon of olive oil. Add the minced garlic and sauté for about 1 minute until fragrant.
Step 3: Add the cherry tomatoes and red bell pepper to the skillet. Cook for 3-4 minutes until the vegetables are tender.
Step 4: Add the spiralized zucchini noodles to the skillet and toss to combine. Cook for 2-3 minutes until the zucchini noodles are just tender.
Step 5: Return the cooked shrimp to the skillet. Add the lemon juice, fresh parsley, and red pepper flakes (if using). Toss everything together and cook for an additional 1-2 minutes until heated through.
Step 6: Adjust seasoning with salt and black pepper to taste. Serve immediately.

This zucchini noodle and shrimp bowl is a quick and easy meal that's packed with protein and fresh vegetables, making it perfect for a nutritious and satisfying lunch.

Nutritional Values: Calories 290 | Carbs 14 g | Protein 30 g | Fiber 4 g | Fat 14 g | Sugar 7 g

4.12 Turkey chili

Preparation Time: 15 min | Cooking Time: 30 min | Servings: 2

Ingredients:
- Ground turkey: 1/2 lb
- Olive oil: 1 tbsp
- Onion: 1 small, diced
- Garlic: 2 cloves, minced
- Red bell pepper: 1/2, diced
- Green bell pepper: 1/2, diced
- Canned diced tomatoes: 1 can (14.5 oz)
- Canned kidney beans: 1 can (15 oz), drained and rinsed
- Chicken broth: 1 cup
- Chili powder: 1 tbsp
- Ground cumin: 1 tsp
- Smoked paprika: 1/2 tsp
- Salt: 1/2 tsp
- Black pepper: 1/4 tsp
- Fresh cilantro: for garnish

Instructions:
Step 1: Heat the olive oil in a large pot over medium heat. Add the diced onion and minced garlic, and sauté until the onion is translucent, about 3-4 minutes.

Step 2: Add the ground turkey to the pot and cook until browned, breaking it up with a spoon as it cooks.
Step 3: Stir in the diced red and green bell peppers, and cook for another 5 minutes until they start to soften.
Step 4: Add the canned diced tomatoes, kidney beans, chicken broth, chili powder, ground cumin, smoked paprika, salt, and black pepper. Stir to combine.
Step 5: Bring the mixture to a boil, then reduce the heat to low and let it simmer for 20 minutes, stirring occasionally.
Step 6: Taste and adjust seasoning if necessary. Serve hot, garnished with fresh cilantro.

This turkey chili is a perfect lunch option that is both hearty and nutritious. It's packed with protein and fiber, making it a satisfying meal that supports blood sugar management.

Nutritional Values: Calories 350 | Carb 35 g | Protein 30 g | Fiber 10 g | Fat 10 g | Sugar 8 g

4.13 Egg salad on rye

Preparation Time: 10 min | Cooking Time: 10 min | Servings: 2

Ingredients:
- Eggs: 4 large
- Rye bread: 4 slices
- Greek yogurt: 1/4 cup
- Dijon mustard: 1 tablespoon
- Celery: 1 stalk, finely chopped
- Red onion: 1/4 small, finely chopped
- Fresh dill: 1 tablespoon, chopped
- Lemon juice: 1 teaspoon
- Salt: 1/4 teaspoon
- Black pepper: 1/4 teaspoon
- Lettuce leaves: 4

Instructions:
Step 1: Place the eggs in a saucepan and cover with water. Bring to a boil, then reduce heat and simmer for 10 minutes. Remove from heat, drain, and cool under cold running water. Peel and chop the eggs.
Step 2: In a medium bowl, combine the Greek yogurt, Dijon mustard, celery, red onion, dill, lemon juice, salt, and black pepper. Mix well.
Step 3: Add the chopped eggs to the bowl and gently fold them into the mixture until well combined.
Step 4: Toast the rye bread slices until golden brown.
Step 5: Place a lettuce leaf on each slice of rye bread, then evenly distribute the egg salad mixture on top of the lettuce.
Step 6: Serve immediately and enjoy!

This egg salad on rye is a perfect blend of creamy and crunchy textures, providing a nutritious and satisfying lunch option that supports blood sugar management. It's quick to prepare and packed with protein and fiber.

Nutritional Values: Calories 300 | Carbs 30 g | Protein 20 g | Fiber 5 g | Fat 15 g | Sugar 5 g

4.14 Balsamic chicken and roasted vegetable salad

Preparation Time: 15 min | Cooking Time: 25 min | Servings: 2

Ingredients:
- Chicken breasts: 2 (about 6 oz each)
- Balsamic vinegar: 1/4 cup
- Olive oil: 3 tbsp (divided)
- Garlic: 2 cloves (minced)
- Mixed baby greens: 4 cups
- Cherry tomatoes: 1 cup (halved)
- Red bell pepper: 1 (sliced)
- Zucchini: 1 (sliced)
- Red onion: 1/2 (sliced)
- Salt: to taste
- Black pepper: to taste
- Feta cheese: 1/4 cup (crumbled)
- Fresh basil: 2 tbsp (chopped)

Instructions:
Step 1: Preheat the oven to 400°F (200°C). In a small bowl, mix balsamic vinegar, 2 tbsp olive oil, minced garlic, salt, and black pepper.
Step 2: Place the chicken breasts in a resealable plastic bag and pour half of the balsamic mixture over the chicken. Seal the bag and marinate in the refrigerator for at least 15 minutes.
Step 3: On a baking sheet, spread the red bell pepper, zucchini, and red onion. Drizzle with 1 tbsp olive oil, and season with salt and black pepper. Roast in the oven for 20-25 minutes, or until vegetables are tender and slightly charred.
Step 4: While the vegetables are roasting, heat a grill pan over medium-high heat. Remove the chicken from the marinade and grill for about 6-7 minutes on each side, or until fully cooked. Let the chicken rest for a few minutes before slicing.
Step 5: In a large bowl, combine mixed baby greens, cherry tomatoes, roasted vegetables, and sliced chicken. Drizzle with the remaining balsamic mixture and toss gently to combine.
Step 6: Top the salad with crumbled feta cheese and chopped fresh basil before serving.

This balsamic chicken and roasted vegetable salad is a perfect blend of flavors and textures, providing a nutritious and satisfying lunch that supports blood sugar management.

Nutritional Values: Calories 400 | Carb 20 g | Protein 35 g | Fiber 6 g | Fat 20 g | Sugar 10 g

4.15 Smoked salmon and cream cheese bagel

Preparation Time: 10 min | Cooking Time: 0 min | Servings: 2

Ingredients:
- Bagels: 2 whole

- Cream cheese: 4 tablespoons
- Smoked salmon: 4 ounces
- Red onion: 1/4 small, thinly sliced
- Capers: 2 tablespoons
- Fresh dill: 2 teaspoons, chopped
- Lemon: 1, cut into wedges
- Black pepper: to taste

Instructions:
Step 1: Slice the bagels in half and toast them to your desired level of crispiness.
Step 2: Spread 2 tablespoons of cream cheese evenly on each bagel half.
Step 3: Layer 2 ounces of smoked salmon on top of the cream cheese on each bagel half.
Step 4: Add a few slices of red onion and a sprinkle of capers on top of the salmon.
Step 5: Garnish with fresh dill and a squeeze of lemon juice.
Step 6: Season with black pepper to taste.

This smoked salmon and cream cheese bagel is a quick and delicious lunch option that is rich in protein and healthy fats, perfect for maintaining balanced blood sugar levels.

Nutritional Values: Calories 350 | Carbs 45 g | Protein 15 g | Fiber 3 g | Fat 15 g | Sugar 6 g

4.16 Beef and vegetable stir-fry

Preparation Time: 10 min | Cooking Time: 10 min | Servings: 2

Ingredients:
- Beef sirloin: 8 oz, thinly sliced
- Broccoli florets: 1 cup
- Red bell pepper: 1, thinly sliced
- Carrot: 1, julienned
- Snow peas: 1/2 cup
- Garlic: 2 cloves, minced
- Fresh ginger: 1 tsp, minced
- Soy sauce: 2 tbsp
- Oyster sauce: 1 tbsp
- Sesame oil: 1 tsp
- Olive oil: 1 tbsp
- Cornstarch: 1 tsp, dissolved in 1 tbsp water
- Green onions: 2, chopped
- Sesame seeds: 1 tsp, for garnish

Instructions:
Step 1: Heat olive oil in a large skillet or wok over medium-high heat.
Step 2: Add the minced garlic and ginger, and stir-fry for about 30 seconds until fragrant.
Step 3: Add the beef slices and stir-fry until browned and cooked through, about 3-4 minutes. Remove beef from the skillet and set aside.

Step 4: In the same skillet, add broccoli, red bell pepper, carrot, and snow peas. Stir-fry for 3-4 minutes until vegetables are tender-crisp.
Step 5: Return the beef to the skillet. Add soy sauce, oyster sauce, and sesame oil. Stir well to combine.
Step 6: Pour in the cornstarch mixture and cook for another 1-2 minutes until the sauce thickens.
Step 7: Garnish with chopped green onions and sesame seeds before serving.

This beef and vegetable stir-fry is a quick and nutritious option for lunch, packed with protein and colorful vegetables to keep you energized throughout the day.

Nutritional Values: Calories 350 | Carb 20 g | Protein 30 g | Fiber 5 g | Fat 15 g | Sugar 5 g

4.17 Caprese salad with grilled chicken

Preparation Time: 15 min | Cooking Time: 15 min | Servings: 2

Ingredients:
- Chicken breast: 2 (about 6 oz each)
- Olive oil: 2 tbsp
- Salt: 1/2 tsp
- Black pepper: 1/2 tsp
- Fresh mozzarella: 4 oz, sliced
- Cherry tomatoes: 1 cup, halved
- Fresh basil leaves: 1/2 cup
- Balsamic glaze: 2 tbsp

Instructions:
Step 1: Preheat the grill to medium-high heat.
Step 2: Brush the chicken breasts with olive oil and season with salt and black pepper.
Step 3: Grill the chicken for about 6-7 minutes on each side, or until fully cooked and no longer pink in the center.
Step 4: While the chicken is grilling, arrange the fresh mozzarella slices, cherry tomatoes, and basil leaves on two plates.
Step 5: Once the chicken is cooked, let it rest for a few minutes before slicing it into strips.
Step 6: Place the grilled chicken strips on top of the mozzarella, tomatoes, and basil.
Step 7: Drizzle the balsamic glaze over the salad and serve immediately.

This vibrant salad combines the freshness of Caprese with the heartiness of grilled chicken, creating a diabetes-friendly meal that's both flavorful and nutrient-rich. Quick to prepare, it's perfect for any healthy eating plan.

Nutritional Values: Calories 400 | Carbs 10 g | Protein 40 g | Fiber 2 g | Fat 20 g | Sugar 6 g

4.18 Butternut squash soup

Preparation Time: 15 min | Cooking Time: 30 min | Servings: 2

Ingredients:
- Butternut squash: 1 small (about 2 cups cubed)
- Olive oil: 1 tablespoon
- Yellow onion: 1 small, chopped
- Garlic: 2 cloves, minced
- Vegetable broth: 2 cups
- Coconut milk: 1/2 cup
- Ground nutmeg: 1/4 teaspoon
- Salt: 1/2 teaspoon
- Black pepper: 1/4 teaspoon
- Fresh thyme: 1 teaspoon, chopped (optional for garnish)

Instructions:

Step 1: Preheat your oven to 400°F (200°C). Peel and cube the butternut squash, then toss with olive oil and spread on a baking sheet. Roast for 25 minutes, or until tender.

Step 2: In a large pot, heat a little olive oil over medium heat. Add the chopped onion and cook until translucent, about 5 minutes. Add the minced garlic and cook for another minute.

Step 3: Add the roasted butternut squash to the pot along with the vegetable broth. Bring to a boil, then reduce heat and simmer for 10 minutes.

Step 4: Use an immersion blender to puree the soup until smooth. Alternatively, transfer the soup to a blender in batches and blend until smooth.

Step 5: Stir in the coconut milk, ground nutmeg, salt, and black pepper. Simmer for another 5 minutes to let the flavors meld.

Step 6: Ladle the soup into bowls and garnish with fresh thyme if desired. Serve hot.

This butternut squash soup is not only delicious but also packed with nutrients. It's a perfect, quick, and satisfying lunch that aligns with the principles of balanced blood sugar management.

Nutritional Values: Calories 200 | Carbs 30 g | Protein 3 g | Fiber 5 g | Fat 10 g | Sugar 6 g

SCAN THE QR CODE
TO ACCESS
YOUR EXCLUSIVE BONUS
info@retoteufel.com

5. Delicious diabetic-friendly dinners
5.1 Grilled chicken with quinoa salad

Preparation Time: 15 min | Cooking Time: 20 min | Servings: 2

Ingredients:
- Chicken breast: 2 (6 oz each)
- Olive oil: 2 tbsp
- Lemon juice: 2 tbsp
- Garlic: 2 cloves, minced
- Dried oregano: 1 tsp
- Salt: 1/2 tsp
- Black pepper: 1/4 tsp
- Quinoa: 1/2 cup, uncooked
- Water: 1 cup
- Cherry tomatoes: 1 cup, halved
- Cucumber: 1, diced
- Red onion: 1/4, finely chopped
- Fresh parsley: 1/4 cup, chopped
- Feta cheese: 1/4 cup, crumbled (optional)
- Balsamic vinegar: 1 tbsp

Instructions:
Step 1: In a small bowl, mix olive oil, lemon juice, minced garlic, dried oregano, salt, and black pepper. Marinate the chicken breasts in this mixture for at least 10 minutes.
Step 2: While the chicken is marinating, rinse the quinoa under cold water. In a medium saucepan, bring water to a boil, add quinoa, reduce heat to low, cover, and simmer for about 15 minutes or until water is absorbed. Fluff with a fork and let it cool.
Step 3: Preheat the grill to medium-high heat. Grill the chicken breasts for about 6-7 minutes on each side or until fully cooked and juices run clear. Remove from grill and let rest for a few minutes before slicing.
Step 4: In a large bowl, combine the cooked quinoa, cherry tomatoes, cucumber, red onion, fresh parsley, and feta cheese (if using). Drizzle with balsamic vinegar and toss to combine.
Step 5: Serve the grilled chicken slices over the quinoa salad.

This grilled chicken with quinoa salad is a perfect blend of lean protein and whole grains, making it an ideal diabetic-friendly dinner. It's quick to prepare and packed with nutrients!

Nutritional Values: Calories 400 | Carbs 35 g | Protein 40 g | Fiber 5 g | Fat 15 g | Sugar 5 g

5.2 Turkey and spinach stuffed peppers

Preparation Time: 15 min | Cooking Time: 30 min | Servings: 2

Ingredients:
- Bell peppers: 2 large
- Ground turkey: 8 oz
- Fresh spinach: 2 cups, chopped
- Onion: 1/2 cup, finely chopped
- Garlic: 2 cloves, minced
- Olive oil: 1 tbsp
- Diced tomatoes: 1/2 cup, no salt added
- Tomato sauce: 1/2 cup, no salt added
- Italian seasoning: 1 tsp
- Salt: 1/4 tsp
- Black pepper: 1/4 tsp
- Low-fat mozzarella cheese: 1/4 cup, shredded

Instructions:
Step 1: Preheat the oven to 375°F (190°C). Cut the tops off the bell peppers and remove the seeds and membranes. Set aside.
Step 2: In a large skillet, heat olive oil over medium heat. Add the onion and garlic, and sauté until softened, about 3 minutes.
Step 3: Add the ground turkey to the skillet and cook until browned, breaking it up with a spoon, about 5 minutes.
Step 4: Stir in the chopped spinach, diced tomatoes, tomato sauce, Italian seasoning, salt, and black pepper. Cook for another 3-4 minutes until the spinach is wilted and the mixture is well combined.
Step 5: Stuff each bell pepper with the turkey and spinach mixture, pressing down to fill completely.
Step 6: Place the stuffed peppers in a baking dish and cover with aluminum foil. Bake in the preheated oven for 25 minutes.
Step 7: Remove the foil, sprinkle the shredded mozzarella cheese on top of each stuffed pepper, and bake for an additional 5 minutes, or until the cheese is melted and bubbly.

This dish is a perfect blend of lean protein and nutrient-rich vegetables, making it a delicious and healthy option for a diabetic-friendly dinner.

Nutritional Values: Calories 280 | Carbs 18 g | Protein 30 g | Fiber 6 g | Fat 10 g | Sugar 8 g

5.3 Baked salmon with steamed broccoli

Preparation Time: 10 min | Cooking Time: 20 min | Servings: 2

Ingredients:
- Salmon fillets: 2 (6 oz each)
- Olive oil: 1 tbsp
- Lemon juice: 1 tbsp
- Garlic: 2 cloves, minced
- Fresh dill: 1 tbsp, chopped
- Salt: 1/2 tsp
- Black pepper: 1/4 tsp
- Broccoli florets: 3 cups
- Water: 1/2 cup

Instructions:
Step 1: Preheat your oven to 400°F (200°C). Line a baking sheet with parchment paper.
Step 2: In a small bowl, mix together the olive oil, lemon juice, minced garlic, chopped dill, salt, and black pepper.
Step 3: Place the salmon fillets on the prepared baking sheet. Brush the olive oil mixture evenly over the salmon fillets.
Step 4: Bake the salmon in the preheated oven for 15-20 minutes, or until the salmon is cooked through and flakes easily with a fork.
Step 5: While the salmon is baking, bring 1/2 cup of water to a boil in a medium saucepan. Add the broccoli florets, cover, and steam for 5-7 minutes, or until tender.
Step 6: Serve the baked salmon with the steamed broccoli on the side. Enjoy your healthy and delicious diabetic-friendly dinner!

This baked salmon with steamed broccoli is not only quick and easy to prepare but also packed with lean protein and essential nutrients, making it a perfect choice for a diabetic-friendly dinner.

Nutritional Values: Calories 350 | Carbs 10 g | Protein 40 g | Fiber 4 g | Fat 18 g | Sugar 3 g

5.4 Vegetarian chili

Preparation Time: 15 min | Cooking Time: 30 min | Servings: 2

Ingredients:
- Olive oil: 1 tablespoon
- Onion: 1 small, diced
- Garlic: 2 cloves, minced
- Bell pepper: 1 medium, diced
- Carrot: 1 medium, diced
- Zucchini: 1 small, diced
- Canned diced tomatoes: 1 can (14.5 oz)
- Canned black beans: 1 can (15 oz), drained and rinsed

- Canned kidney beans: 1 can (15 oz), drained and rinsed
- Tomato paste: 2 tablespoons
- Vegetable broth: 1 cup
- Chili powder: 1 tablespoon
- Ground cumin: 1 teaspoon
- Paprika: 1 teaspoon
- Oregano: 1 teaspoon
- Salt: 1/2 teaspoon
- Black pepper: 1/4 teaspoon
- Fresh cilantro: 2 tablespoons, chopped (optional)

Instructions:
Step 1: Heat the olive oil in a large pot over medium heat. Add the diced onion and minced garlic, and sauté until the onion is translucent, about 3-4 minutes.
Step 2: Add the diced bell pepper, carrot, and zucchini to the pot. Cook for another 5 minutes, stirring occasionally, until the vegetables start to soften.
Step 3: Stir in the canned diced tomatoes, black beans, kidney beans, tomato paste, and vegetable broth.
Step 4: Add the chili powder, ground cumin, paprika, oregano, salt, and black pepper. Stir well to combine all the ingredients.
Step 5: Bring the mixture to a boil, then reduce the heat to low. Cover and let it simmer for 20 minutes, stirring occasionally.
Step 6: Taste and adjust the seasoning if needed. If using, stir in the chopped fresh cilantro just before serving.

This vegetarian chili is not only delicious but also packed with fiber and protein, making it a perfect diabetic-friendly dinner option. It's quick to prepare and full of flavor, ensuring a satisfying meal without compromising dietary needs.

Nutritional Values: Calories 350 | Carb 60 g | Protein 18 g | Fiber 16 g | Fat 8 g | Sugar 10 g

5.5 Beef and vegetable stir-fry

Preparation Time: 15 min | Cooking Time: 15 min | Servings: 2

Ingredients:
- Lean beef (sirloin or tenderloin), thinly sliced: 8 oz
- Olive oil: 1 tbsp
- Low-sodium soy sauce: 2 tbsp
- Fresh ginger, minced: 1 tsp
- Garlic, minced: 2 cloves
- Red bell pepper, thinly sliced: 1
- Broccoli florets: 1 cup
- Carrot, julienned: 1
- Snow peas: 1/2 cup
- Green onions, chopped: 2
- Sesame seeds: 1 tsp (optional)
- Brown rice, cooked: 1 cup

Instructions:
Step 1: Heat olive oil in a large skillet or wok over medium-high heat.
Step 2: Add the minced garlic and ginger, and sauté for about 1 minute until fragrant.
Step 3: Add the thinly sliced beef to the skillet and cook until browned, about 3-4 minutes.
Step 4: Remove the beef from the skillet and set aside.
Step 5: In the same skillet, add the red bell pepper, broccoli, carrot, and snow peas. Stir-fry for about 5 minutes until the vegetables are tender-crisp.
Step 6: Return the beef to the skillet and add the low-sodium soy sauce. Stir well to combine.
Step 7: Cook for an additional 2-3 minutes until everything is heated through.
Step 8: Garnish with chopped green onions and sesame seeds if desired.
Step 9: Serve the stir-fry over cooked brown rice.

This beef and vegetable stir-fry is a quick and nutritious dinner option, perfect for those managing diabetes. It's packed with lean protein and a variety of colorful vegetables, making it both delicious and healthy.

Nutritional Values: Calories 350 | Carbs 30 g | Protein 30 g | Fiber 5 g | Fat 12 g | Sugar 6 g

5.6 Lentil and mushroom stew

Preparation Time: 15 min | Cooking Time: 45 min | Servings: 2

Ingredients:
- Olive oil: 1 tablespoon
- Onion: 1 small, finely chopped
- Garlic: 2 cloves, minced
- Carrots: 2 medium, diced
- Celery: 2 stalks, diced
- Mushrooms: 8 ounces, sliced
- Dried thyme: 1 teaspoon
- Dried rosemary: 1 teaspoon
- Bay leaf: 1
- Green lentils: 1/2 cup, rinsed
- Low-sodium vegetable broth: 3 cups
- Tomato paste: 1 tablespoon
- Baby spinach: 2 cups
- Salt: to taste
- Black pepper: to taste

Instructions:
Step 1: Heat the olive oil in a large pot over medium heat. Add the onion and garlic, and sauté until softened, about 3-4 minutes.
Step 2: Add the carrots and celery, and cook for another 5 minutes, stirring occasionally.
Step 3: Stir in the mushrooms, thyme, rosemary, and bay leaf. Cook until the mushrooms are tender, about 5 minutes.
Step 4: Add the lentils, vegetable broth, and tomato paste. Bring to a boil, then reduce the heat and simmer for

30 minutes, or until the lentils are tender.
Step 5: Stir in the baby spinach and cook until wilted, about 2 minutes. Season with salt and black pepper to taste.
Step 6: Remove the bay leaf before serving.

This hearty lentil and mushroom stew is not only delicious but also packed with nutrients, making it a perfect diabetic-friendly dinner option. It's easy to prepare and full of flavor, ensuring a satisfying meal without compromising your dietary needs.

Nutritional Values: Calories 270 | Carbs 40 g | Protein 15 g | Fiber 15 g | Fat 7 g | Sugar 7 g

5.7 Cauliflower rice and shrimp bowl

Preparation Time: 10 min | Cooking Time: 10 min | Servings: 2

Ingredients:
- Cauliflower: 1 small head, grated into rice-sized pieces
- Shrimp: 8 oz, peeled and deveined
- Olive oil: 2 tbsp
- Garlic: 2 cloves, minced
- Red bell pepper: 1, diced
- Green onions: 2, sliced
- Soy sauce (low sodium): 2 tbsp
- Lime juice: 1 tbsp
- Fresh cilantro: 2 tbsp, chopped
- Salt: to taste
- Black pepper: to taste

Instructions:
Step 1: Heat 1 tablespoon of olive oil in a large skillet over medium heat. Add the shrimp and cook for 2-3 minutes on each side until pink and opaque. Remove shrimp from the skillet and set aside.
Step 2: In the same skillet, add the remaining tablespoon of olive oil. Add the minced garlic and cook for 1 minute until fragrant.
Step 3: Add the grated cauliflower, diced red bell pepper, and sliced green onions to the skillet. Stir-fry for 5-7 minutes until the cauliflower is tender.
Step 4: Return the cooked shrimp to the skillet. Add the soy sauce and lime juice, stirring to combine. Cook for an additional 2 minutes to heat through.
Step 5: Season with salt and black pepper to taste. Garnish with fresh cilantro before serving.

This cauliflower rice and shrimp bowl is a quick, nutritious, and flavorful meal perfect for a diabetic-friendly diet. It's low in carbs, high in protein, and packed with vegetables.

Nutritional Values: Calories 250 | Carbs 15 g | Protein 25 g | Fiber 5 g | Fat 12 g | Sugar 5 g

5.8 Spaghetti squash with turkey meatballs

Preparation Time: 15 min | Cooking Time: 45 min | Servings: 2

Ingredients:
- Spaghetti squash: 1 small (about 2 lbs)
- Ground turkey: 8 oz (lean)
- Egg: 1 large
- Almond flour: 1/4 cup
- Parmesan cheese: 2 tbsp (grated)
- Garlic: 2 cloves (minced)
- Italian seasoning: 1 tsp
- Salt: 1/2 tsp
- Black pepper: 1/4 tsp
- Olive oil: 1 tbsp
- Marinara sauce: 1 cup (no added sugar)
- Fresh basil: for garnish (optional)

Instructions:
Step 1: Preheat your oven to 400°F (200°C). Cut the spaghetti squash in half lengthwise and scoop out the seeds. Place the halves cut-side down on a baking sheet and bake for 40 minutes or until the flesh is tender.
Step 2: While the squash is baking, prepare the turkey meatballs. In a large bowl, combine the ground turkey, egg, almond flour, Parmesan cheese, minced garlic, Italian seasoning, salt, and black pepper. Mix until well combined.
Step 3: Form the mixture into small meatballs, about 1 inch in diameter.
Step 4: Heat the olive oil in a large skillet over medium heat. Add the meatballs and cook until browned on all sides and cooked through, about 10 minutes.
Step 5: Add the marinara sauce to the skillet with the meatballs and simmer for an additional 5 minutes.
Step 6: Once the spaghetti squash is done, use a fork to scrape out the flesh into spaghetti-like strands.
Step 7: Divide the spaghetti squash between two plates and top with the turkey meatballs and marinara sauce. Garnish with fresh basil if desired.

This dish is a perfect low-carb alternative to traditional spaghetti and meatballs, packed with lean protein and fiber, making it a great option for managing diabetes.

Nutritional Values: Calories 350 | Carbs 30 g | Protein 30 g | Fiber 6 g | Fat 15 g | Sugar 8 g

5.9 Grilled vegetable platter with herb dressing

Preparation Time: 15 min | Cooking Time: 20 min | Servings: 2

Ingredients:
- Zucchini: 1 medium, sliced
- Bell peppers: 2 (1 red, 1 yellow), sliced
- Eggplant: 1 small, sliced
- Cherry tomatoes: 1 cup, halved

- Olive oil: 2 tablespoons
- Salt: 1/2 teaspoon
- Black pepper: 1/4 teaspoon
- Fresh basil: 1/4 cup, chopped
- Fresh parsley: 1/4 cup, chopped
- Lemon juice: 1 tablespoon
- Garlic: 2 cloves, minced

Instructions:
Step 1: Preheat the grill to medium-high heat.
Step 2: In a large bowl, toss the zucchini, bell peppers, eggplant, and cherry tomatoes with 1 tablespoon of olive oil, salt, and black pepper.
Step 3: Grill the vegetables for 4-5 minutes on each side or until tender and slightly charred.
Step 4: While the vegetables are grilling, prepare the herb dressing by mixing the remaining olive oil, fresh basil, fresh parsley, lemon juice, and minced garlic in a small bowl.
Step 5: Once the vegetables are done, arrange them on a platter and drizzle with the herb dressing.
Step 6: Serve immediately and enjoy!

This grilled vegetable platter is not only vibrant and flavorful but also packed with nutrients. It's a quick and easy dish that aligns perfectly with a diabetic-friendly diet, offering a healthy balance of fiber, vitamins, and antioxidants.

Nutritional Values: Calories 150 | Carbs 18 g | Protein 3 g | Fiber 6 g | Fat 9 g | Sugar 10 g

5.10 Pork tenderloin with apple cider glaze

Preparation Time: 15 min | Cooking Time: 25 min | Servings: 2

Ingredients:
- Pork tenderloin: 1 (about 12 oz)
- Olive oil: 1 tbsp
- Salt: 1/2 tsp
- Black pepper: 1/4 tsp
- Apple cider: 1/2 cup
- Dijon mustard: 1 tbsp
- Garlic: 2 cloves, minced
- Fresh thyme: 1 tsp, chopped
- Apple: 1, thinly sliced
- Chicken broth: 1/4 cup

Instructions:
Step 1: Preheat the oven to 400°F (200°C). Season the pork tenderloin with salt and black pepper.
Step 2: In an oven-safe skillet, heat the olive oil over medium-high heat. Sear the pork tenderloin on all sides until browned, about 2-3 minutes per side.
Step 3: Remove the pork from the skillet and set aside. In the same skillet, add the minced garlic and cook for 1 minute until fragrant.

Step 4: Add the apple cider, Dijon mustard, and chicken broth to the skillet, stirring to combine. Bring the mixture to a simmer.
Step 5: Return the pork tenderloin to the skillet, spoon some of the glaze over the top, and add the sliced apple around the pork.
Step 6: Transfer the skillet to the preheated oven and roast for 15-20 minutes, or until the internal temperature of the pork reaches 145°F (63°C).
Step 7: Remove the skillet from the oven and let the pork rest for 5 minutes before slicing. Serve with the apple slices and glaze.

This dish is a perfect balance of lean protein and natural sweetness from the apples, making it a delicious and diabetic-friendly dinner option.

Nutritional Values: Calories 300 | Carb 15 g | Protein 30 g | Fiber 2 g | Fat 12 g | Sugar 10 g

5.11 Zucchini noodles with basil pesto

Preparation Time: 10 min | Cooking Time: 10 min | Servings: 2

Ingredients:
- Zucchini: 2 medium-sized
- Fresh basil leaves: 1 cup
- Pine nuts: 1/4 cup
- Parmesan cheese: 1/4 cup, grated
- Garlic: 1 clove
- Extra virgin olive oil: 1/4 cup
- Lemon juice: 1 tbsp
- Salt: to taste
- Black pepper: to taste

Instructions:
Step 1: Using a spiralizer, create zucchini noodles from the zucchini and set aside.
Step 2: In a food processor, combine the basil leaves, pine nuts, Parmesan cheese, and garlic. Pulse until finely chopped.
Step 3: With the food processor running, slowly add the olive oil and lemon juice until the mixture is smooth and creamy. Season with salt and black pepper to taste.
Step 4: In a large bowl, toss the zucchini noodles with the basil pesto until evenly coated.
Step 5: Serve immediately, garnished with additional Parmesan cheese and pine nuts if desired.

This dish is a perfect low-carb, diabetic-friendly dinner option that is both delicious and easy to prepare. The fresh basil pesto adds a burst of flavor, making it a satisfying meal.

Nutritional Values: Calories 250 | Carbs 8 g | Protein 6 g | Fiber 3 g | Fat 22 g | Sugar 4 g

5.12 Chicken tikka masala with cauliflower

Preparation Time: 15 min | Cooking Time: 25 min | Servings: 2

Ingredients:
- Chicken breast: 1 (about 8 oz), cut into bite-sized pieces
- Greek yogurt: 1/2 cup
- Lemon juice: 1 tbsp
- Garlic: 2 cloves, minced
- Ginger: 1 tsp, minced
- Ground cumin: 1 tsp
- Ground coriander: 1 tsp
- Ground turmeric: 1/2 tsp
- Ground paprika: 1/2 tsp
- Ground garam masala: 1 tsp
- Salt: 1/2 tsp
- Olive oil: 1 tbsp
- Onion: 1 small, finely chopped
- Tomato paste: 2 tbsp
- Diced tomatoes: 1 can (14.5 oz)
- Heavy cream: 1/4 cup
- Fresh cilantro: 2 tbsp, chopped
- Cauliflower: 1 small head, cut into florets

Instructions:
Step 1: In a bowl, combine the chicken pieces, Greek yogurt, lemon juice, garlic, ginger, ground cumin, ground coriander, ground turmeric, ground paprika, ground garam masala, and salt. Mix well and let it marinate for at least 30 minutes.
Step 2: Heat the olive oil in a large skillet over medium heat. Add the chopped onion and sauté until golden brown.
Step 3: Add the marinated chicken to the skillet and cook until the chicken is browned on all sides.
Step 4: Stir in the tomato paste and diced tomatoes. Bring to a simmer and cook for about 10 minutes, until the sauce thickens.
Step 5: While the chicken is cooking, steam the cauliflower florets until tender, about 5-7 minutes.
Step 6: Stir the heavy cream into the chicken mixture and cook for an additional 5 minutes.
Step 7: Serve the chicken tikka masala over the steamed cauliflower florets. Garnish with fresh cilantro.

This chicken tikka masala with cauliflower is a flavorful and satisfying dish that is perfect for a diabetic-friendly dinner. The cauliflower provides a low-carb alternative to rice, making it a healthy and delicious choice.

Nutritional Values: Calories 350 | Carb 18 g | Protein 35 g | Fiber 5 g | Fat 15 g | Sugar 9 g

5.13 Eggplant and chickpea tagine

Preparation Time: 15 min | Cooking Time: 45 min | Servings: 2

Ingredients:
- Eggplant: 1 medium, diced
- Chickpeas: 1 can (15 oz), drained and rinsed
- Olive oil: 2 tbsp
- Onion: 1 small, finely chopped
- Garlic: 2 cloves, minced
- Ground cumin: 1 tsp
- Ground coriander: 1 tsp
- Ground cinnamon: 1/2 tsp
- Ground turmeric: 1/2 tsp
- Diced tomatoes: 1 can (14.5 oz)
- Low-sodium vegetable broth: 1 cup
- Fresh cilantro: 1/4 cup, chopped
- Salt: to taste
- Black pepper: to taste

Instructions:
Step 1: Heat the olive oil in a large pot over medium heat. Add the chopped onion and minced garlic, and sauté until the onion is translucent, about 5 minutes.
Step 2: Stir in the ground cumin, ground coriander, ground cinnamon, and ground turmeric. Cook for an additional 1-2 minutes until the spices are fragrant.
Step 3: Add the diced eggplant to the pot and cook for about 5 minutes, stirring occasionally, until the eggplant starts to soften.
Step 4: Pour in the diced tomatoes and vegetable broth, and bring the mixture to a simmer.
Step 5: Add the drained chickpeas to the pot, and season with salt and black pepper to taste. Cover and let the tagine simmer for about 30 minutes, or until the eggplant is tender and the flavors have melded together.
Step 6: Stir in the chopped fresh cilantro just before serving.

This eggplant and chickpea tagine is a hearty and flavorful dish that is perfect for a diabetic-friendly dinner. It's packed with fiber and protein, making it both satisfying and nutritious.

Nutritional Values: Calories 280 | Carb 40 g | Protein 10 g | Fiber 12 g | Fat 10 g | Sugar 10 g

5.14 Baked cod with olive tapenade

Preparation Time: 10 min | Cooking Time: 20 min | Servings: 2

Ingredients:
- Cod fillets: 2 (6 oz each)
- Olive oil: 1 tbsp
- Lemon juice: 1 tbsp
- Garlic: 2 cloves, minced
- Kalamata olives: 1/4 cup, pitted and chopped
- Capers: 1 tbsp, rinsed and chopped
- Fresh parsley: 2 tbsp, chopped

- Black pepper: to taste
- Salt: to taste

Instructions:
Step 1: Preheat your oven to 400°F (200°C). Line a baking sheet with parchment paper.
Step 2: In a small bowl, combine the olive oil, lemon juice, minced garlic, chopped olives, capers, and parsley. Mix well to create the tapenade.
Step 3: Place the cod fillets on the prepared baking sheet. Season them with salt and black pepper to taste.
Step 4: Spread the olive tapenade evenly over the top of each cod fillet.
Step 5: Bake in the preheated oven for 15-20 minutes, or until the cod is opaque and flakes easily with a fork.
Step 6: Serve the baked cod with a side of steamed vegetables or a fresh salad for a complete diabetic-friendly meal.

This baked cod with olive tapenade is not only delicious but also packed with lean protein and healthy fats, making it an excellent choice for a diabetic-friendly dinner. The recipe is quick and easy to prepare, perfect for a nutritious weeknight meal.

Nutritional Values: Calories 250 | Carb 3 g | Protein 35 g | Fiber 1 g | Fat 10 g | Sugar 0 g

5.15 Tofu and vegetable curry

Preparation Time: 15 min | Cooking Time: 25 min | Servings: 2

Ingredients:
- Extra-firm tofu: 8 oz, cubed
- Olive oil: 1 tbsp
- Onion: 1 small, finely chopped
- Garlic: 2 cloves, minced
- Ginger: 1 inch piece, grated
- Red bell pepper: 1 small, diced
- Zucchini: 1 small, sliced
- Carrot: 1 small, sliced
- Coconut milk (light): 1 cup
- Low-sodium vegetable broth: 1/2 cup
- Curry powder: 1 tbsp
- Ground cumin: 1 tsp
- Ground coriander: 1 tsp
- Turmeric: 1/2 tsp
- Salt: 1/4 tsp
- Black pepper: 1/4 tsp
- Fresh cilantro: 2 tbsp, chopped
- Lime: 1, cut into wedges (optional)

Instructions:
Step 1: Heat the olive oil in a large skillet over medium heat. Add the onion, garlic, and ginger, and sauté until the onion is translucent, about 3-4 minutes.

Step 2: Add the red bell pepper, zucchini, and carrot to the skillet. Cook for another 5 minutes, stirring occasionally.
Step 3: Stir in the curry powder, ground cumin, ground coriander, turmeric, salt, and black pepper. Cook for 1 minute until fragrant.
Step 4: Pour in the coconut milk and vegetable broth. Bring to a simmer.
Step 5: Add the cubed tofu to the skillet and gently stir to combine. Simmer for 10-15 minutes until the vegetables are tender and the flavors have melded together.
Step 6: Garnish with fresh cilantro and serve with lime wedges on the side, if desired.

This tofu and vegetable curry is a delightful, nutrient-rich dish that's perfect for a diabetic-friendly dinner. It's quick to prepare, full of flavor, and packed with protein and fiber.

Nutritional Values: Calories 280 | Carbs 20 g | Protein 12 g | Fiber 5 g | Fat 18 g | Sugar 6 g

5.16 Stuffed acorn squash

Preparation Time: 15 min | Cooking Time: 45 min | Servings: 2

Ingredients:
- Acorn squash: 1 medium
- Olive oil: 1 tbsp
- Ground turkey: 1/2 lb
- Onion: 1/2 cup, finely chopped
- Garlic: 2 cloves, minced
- Spinach: 1 cup, chopped
- Quinoa: 1/2 cup, cooked
- Dried cranberries: 2 tbsp
- Feta cheese: 1/4 cup, crumbled
- Salt: 1/2 tsp
- Black pepper: 1/4 tsp
- Fresh parsley: 2 tbsp, chopped

Instructions:
Step 1: Preheat the oven to 400°F (200°C). Cut the acorn squash in half and scoop out the seeds. Brush the insides with olive oil and place cut-side down on a baking sheet. Roast for 30-35 minutes until tender.
Step 2: While the squash is roasting, heat a skillet over medium heat. Add the ground turkey and cook until browned, about 5-7 minutes. Add the onion and garlic, and sauté until softened, about 3 minutes.
Step 3: Stir in the spinach and cook until wilted. Add the cooked quinoa, dried cranberries, feta cheese, salt, and black pepper. Mix well and cook for another 2-3 minutes.
Step 4: Remove the squash from the oven and flip them over. Fill each half with the turkey mixture. Return to the oven and bake for an additional 10 minutes.
Step 5: Garnish with fresh parsley before serving.

This stuffed acorn squash is a delightful combination of flavors and textures, perfect for a nutritious and satisfying diabetic-friendly dinner. It's easy to prepare and packed with protein, fiber, and essential nutrients.

Nutritional Values: Calories 350 | Carb 40 g | Protein 25 g | Fiber 8 g | Fat 12 g | Sugar 10 g

5.17 Chicken and barley soup

Preparation Time: 15 min | Cooking Time: 45 min | Servings: 2

Ingredients:
- Olive oil: 1 tablespoon
- Chicken breast, boneless and skinless: 1 (about 6 oz), diced
- Onion: 1 small, finely chopped
- Carrot: 1 medium, diced
- Celery stalk: 1, diced
- Garlic: 2 cloves, minced
- Low-sodium chicken broth: 4 cups
- Pearl barley: 1/4 cup
- Dried thyme: 1/2 teaspoon
- Dried rosemary: 1/2 teaspoon
- Bay leaf: 1
- Fresh spinach: 2 cups, roughly chopped
- Salt: to taste
- Black pepper: to taste

Instructions:
Step 1: Heat the olive oil in a large pot over medium heat. Add the diced chicken and cook until browned, about 5-7 minutes. Remove the chicken and set aside.
Step 2: In the same pot, add the chopped onion, carrot, and celery. Sauté until the vegetables are tender, about 5 minutes. Add the minced garlic and cook for another minute.
Step 3: Pour in the chicken broth and bring to a boil. Stir in the barley, thyme, rosemary, and bay leaf. Reduce the heat to low and let it simmer for 30 minutes.
Step 4: Return the cooked chicken to the pot and add the chopped spinach. Simmer for an additional 5 minutes until the spinach is wilted and the chicken is heated through.
Step 5: Season with salt and black pepper to taste. Remove the bay leaf before serving.

This hearty chicken and barley soup is not only delicious but also packed with nutrients. It's a perfect dinner option for managing diabetes, featuring lean protein, whole grains, and plenty of vegetables.

Nutritional Values: Calories 250 | Carb 30 g | Protein 25 g | Fiber 6 g | Fat 5 g | Sugar 4 g

5.18 Roasted turkey with garlic green beans

Preparation Time: 15 min | Cooking Time: 40 min | Servings: 2

Ingredients:
- Turkey breast: 1 lb

- Olive oil: 2 tbsp
- Garlic cloves: 4, minced
- Fresh green beans: 1/2 lb, trimmed
- Lemon juice: 1 tbsp
- Salt: 1/2 tsp
- Black pepper: 1/4 tsp
- Fresh parsley: 1 tbsp, chopped (optional)

Instructions:

Step 1: Preheat your oven to 375°F (190°C).
Step 2: Rub the turkey breast with 1 tbsp of olive oil, 2 minced garlic cloves, salt, and black pepper.
Step 3: Place the turkey breast on a baking sheet and roast in the preheated oven for 25-30 minutes, or until the internal temperature reaches 165°F (74°C).
Step 4: While the turkey is roasting, heat the remaining 1 tbsp of olive oil in a large skillet over medium heat.
Step 5: Add the remaining minced garlic and sauté for 1-2 minutes until fragrant.
Step 6: Add the green beans to the skillet and sauté for 5-7 minutes until tender-crisp.
Step 7: Drizzle the lemon juice over the green beans and season with a pinch of salt and pepper.
Step 8: Remove the turkey from the oven and let it rest for 5 minutes before slicing.
Step 9: Serve the sliced turkey breast with the garlic green beans, garnished with fresh parsley if desired.

This roasted turkey with garlic green beans is a perfect diabetic-friendly dinner. It's rich in lean protein, low in carbs, and packed with flavor, making it both nutritious and delicious.

Nutritional Values: Calories 320 | Carbs 10 g | Protein 45 g | Fiber 4 g | Fat 12 g | Sugar 2 g

SCAN THE QR CODE
TO ACCESS
YOUR EXCLUSIVE BONUS
info@retoteufel.com

6. Salads full of flavor

6.1 Spinach and strawberry salad

Preparation Time: 10 min | Cooking Time: 0 min | Servings: 2

Ingredients:
- Fresh spinach: 4 cups
- Fresh strawberries: 1 cup, sliced
- Red onion: 1/4 cup, thinly sliced
- Feta cheese: 1/4 cup, crumbled
- Sliced almonds: 1/4 cup, toasted
- Balsamic vinaigrette: 3 tablespoons

Instructions:
Step 1: In a large salad bowl, combine the fresh spinach, sliced strawberries, and thinly sliced red onion.
Step 2: Sprinkle the crumbled feta cheese and toasted sliced almonds over the salad mixture.
Step 3: Drizzle the balsamic vinaigrette over the salad and toss gently to combine all ingredients evenly.

This spinach and strawberry salad is a delightful combination of sweet and savory flavors, perfect for a quick and nutritious meal. It's low in carbohydrates and high in fiber, making it an ideal choice for a healthy diet.

Nutritional Values: Calories 220 | Carb 18 g | Protein 6 g | Fiber 4 g | Fat 15 g | Sugar 10 g

6.2 Grilled chicken caesar with kale

Preparation Time: 15 min | Cooking Time: 15 min | Servings: 2

Ingredients:
- Chicken breast: 2 (about 8 oz each)
- Olive oil: 2 tbsp
- Salt: 1/2 tsp
- Black pepper: 1/2 tsp

- Kale: 4 cups, chopped
- Romaine lettuce: 2 cups, chopped
- Parmesan cheese: 1/4 cup, grated
- Caesar dressing: 1/4 cup
- Lemon juice: 1 tbsp
- Garlic: 1 clove, minced
- Croutons: 1/2 cup

Instructions:
Step 1: Preheat the grill to medium-high heat.
Step 2: Brush the chicken breasts with olive oil and season with salt and black pepper.
Step 3: Grill the chicken breasts for about 6-7 minutes on each side, or until fully cooked. Remove from grill and let rest for 5 minutes, then slice thinly.
Step 4: In a large bowl, combine the chopped kale and romaine lettuce.
Step 5: In a small bowl, mix the Caesar dressing, lemon juice, and minced garlic.
Step 6: Pour the dressing over the kale and romaine, and toss to coat evenly.
Step 7: Divide the salad between two plates, top with sliced grilled chicken, grated Parmesan cheese, and croutons.

This grilled chicken Caesar with kale is a delicious and nutritious twist on the classic Caesar salad. It's packed with protein and fiber, making it a satisfying meal that's perfect for a healthy diet.

Nutritional Values: Calories 450 | Carbs 15 g | Protein 38 g | Fiber 6 g | Fat 28 g | Sugar 2 g

6.3 Mediterranean chickpea salad

Preparation Time: 15 min | Cooking Time: 0 min | Servings: 2

Ingredients:
- Chickpeas (cooked): 1 cup
- Cherry tomatoes (halved): 1 cup
- Cucumber (diced): 1 cup
- Red onion (finely chopped): 1/4 cup
- Kalamata olives (sliced): 1/4 cup
- Feta cheese (crumbled): 1/4 cup
- Fresh parsley (chopped): 2 tablespoons
- Extra virgin olive oil: 2 tablespoons
- Lemon juice: 1 tablespoon
- Red wine vinegar: 1 teaspoon
- Garlic (minced): 1 clove
- Salt: to taste
- Black pepper: to taste

Instructions:
Step 1: In a large bowl, combine the chickpeas, cherry tomatoes, cucumber, red onion, Kalamata olives, feta cheese, and fresh parsley.

Step 2: In a small bowl, whisk together the extra virgin olive oil, lemon juice, red wine vinegar, minced garlic, salt, and black pepper.
Step 3: Pour the dressing over the salad and toss gently to combine.
Step 4: Let the salad sit for about 10 minutes to allow the flavors to meld together before serving.

This Mediterranean Chickpea Salad is a vibrant and nutritious dish, perfect for a quick and healthy meal. It's packed with fiber and protein, making it a satisfying option for those looking to maintain a balanced diet.

Nutritional Values: Calories 300 | Carb 35 g | Protein 10 g | Fiber 10 g | Fat 15 g | Sugar 5 g

6.4 Quinoa and black bean salad

Preparation Time: 10 min | Cooking Time: 10 min | Servings: 2

Ingredients:
- Quinoa: 1/2 cup
- Water: 1 cup
- Black beans: 1 cup (canned, drained, and rinsed)
- Red bell pepper: 1/2 cup (diced)
- Corn kernels: 1/2 cup (canned or fresh)
- Red onion: 1/4 cup (finely chopped)
- Cilantro: 1/4 cup (chopped)
- Lime juice: 2 tablespoons
- Olive oil: 1 tablespoon
- Cumin: 1/2 teaspoon
- Salt: 1/4 teaspoon
- Black pepper: 1/4 teaspoon

Instructions:
Step 1: Rinse the quinoa under cold water. In a medium saucepan, combine the quinoa and water. Bring to a boil, then reduce the heat to low, cover, and simmer for about 10 minutes or until the quinoa is tender and the water is absorbed. Fluff with a fork and let it cool.
Step 2: In a large bowl, combine the cooked quinoa, black beans, red bell pepper, corn, red onion, and cilantro.
Step 3: In a small bowl, whisk together the lime juice, olive oil, cumin, salt, and black pepper.
Step 4: Pour the dressing over the quinoa mixture and toss to combine. Adjust seasoning if necessary.
Step 5: Serve immediately or refrigerate for up to 2 hours to let the flavors meld.

This quinoa and black bean salad is a vibrant, protein-packed dish that's both delicious and nutritious. It's quick to prepare and perfect for a healthy, fiber-rich meal.

Nutritional Values: Calories 320 | Carbs 50 g | Protein 12 g | Fiber 10 g | Fat 10 g | Sugar 4 g

6.5 Beetroot and goat cheese salad

Preparation Time: 15 min | Cooking Time: 30 min | Servings: 2

Ingredients:
- Beetroot: 2 medium, roasted and diced
- Goat cheese: 4 oz, crumbled
- Mixed greens: 4 cups
- Walnuts: 1/4 cup, toasted and chopped
- Balsamic vinegar: 2 tbsp
- Olive oil: 2 tbsp
- Honey: 1 tsp
- Salt: to taste
- Black pepper: to taste

Instructions:
Step 1: Preheat the oven to 400°F (200°C). Wrap the beetroots in aluminum foil and roast for 30 minutes or until tender. Let them cool, then peel and dice.
Step 2: In a small bowl, whisk together the balsamic vinegar, olive oil, honey, salt, and black pepper to make the dressing.
Step 3: In a large bowl, combine the mixed greens, roasted beetroot, crumbled goat cheese, and toasted walnuts.
Step 4: Drizzle the dressing over the salad and toss gently to combine.
Step 5: Serve immediately, ensuring each plate has an even distribution of ingredients.

This beetroot and goat cheese salad is a delightful blend of earthy, sweet, and tangy flavors, perfect for a nutritious and satisfying meal. It's quick to prepare and packed with fiber and healthy fats, making it an excellent choice for a balanced diet.

Nutritional Values: Calories 300 | Carb 22 g | Protein 10 g | Fiber 6 g | Fat 22 g | Sugar 14 g

6.6 Asian tofu salad

Preparation Time: 15 min | Cooking Time: 10 min | Servings: 2

Ingredients:
- Extra-firm tofu: 8 oz, drained and cubed
- Soy sauce: 2 tbsp
- Sesame oil: 1 tbsp
- Rice vinegar: 1 tbsp
- Honey: 1 tsp
- Garlic: 1 clove, minced
- Fresh ginger: 1 tsp, grated
- Mixed salad greens: 4 cups
- Red bell pepper: 1, thinly sliced
- Carrot: 1, julienned
- Cucumber: 1/2, thinly sliced
- Green onions: 2, chopped
- Cilantro: 1/4 cup, chopped
- Sesame seeds: 1 tbsp, toasted

Instructions:
Step 1: In a bowl, combine soy sauce, sesame oil, rice vinegar, honey, garlic, and ginger. Mix well to create the dressing.
Step 2: Add the cubed tofu to the dressing and let it marinate for at least 10 minutes.
Step 3: Heat a non-stick skillet over medium heat. Add the marinated tofu and cook for about 5-7 minutes, turning occasionally until golden brown.
Step 4: In a large salad bowl, combine the mixed salad greens, red bell pepper, carrot, cucumber, green onions, and cilantro.
Step 5: Add the cooked tofu to the salad and toss gently to combine.
Step 6: Sprinkle the toasted sesame seeds on top before serving.

This Asian tofu salad is a delightful blend of fresh vegetables and flavorful tofu, making it a perfect low-carb, high-fiber meal. Quick to prepare and packed with nutrients, it's an excellent choice for a healthy lifestyle.

Nutritional Values: Calories 220 | Carbs 18 g | Protein 14 g | Fiber 6 g | Fat 12 g | Sugar 6 g

6.7 Turkey and cranberry salad

Preparation Time: 15 min | Cooking Time: 10 min | Servings: 2

Ingredients:
- Cooked turkey breast: 1 cup, shredded
- Fresh cranberries: 1/2 cup
- Mixed greens: 4 cups
- Red onion: 1/4 cup, thinly sliced
- Celery: 1/2 cup, chopped
- Walnuts: 1/4 cup, chopped
- Feta cheese: 1/4 cup, crumbled
- Olive oil: 2 tablespoons
- Balsamic vinegar: 1 tablespoon
- Honey: 1 teaspoon
- Salt: to taste
- Black pepper: to taste

Instructions:
Step 1: In a small bowl, whisk together the olive oil, balsamic vinegar, honey, salt, and black pepper to make the dressing.
Step 2: In a large salad bowl, combine the mixed greens, shredded turkey, fresh cranberries, red onion, celery, walnuts, and feta cheese.
Step 3: Drizzle the dressing over the salad and toss gently to combine all ingredients evenly.
Step 4: Serve immediately and enjoy this flavorful and nutritious salad.

This turkey and cranberry salad is a delightful combination of savory and sweet flavors, perfect for a quick and healthy meal. It's packed with protein and fiber, making it a satisfying option for any time of the day.

Nutritional Values: Calories 320 | Carb 20 g | Protein 25 g | Fiber 6 g | Fat 18 g | Sugar 10 g

6.8 Cucumber and dill salad

Preparation Time: 10 min | **Cooking Time:** 0 min | **Servings:** 2

Ingredients:
- Cucumber: 1 large, thinly sliced
- Fresh dill: 2 tablespoons, chopped
- Red onion: 1/4 small, thinly sliced
- Greek yogurt: 1/4 cup
- Lemon juice: 1 tablespoon
- Olive oil: 1 teaspoon
- Salt: 1/4 teaspoon
- Black pepper: 1/8 teaspoon

Instructions:
Step 1: In a large bowl, combine the thinly sliced cucumber, chopped dill, and thinly sliced red onion.
Step 2: In a small bowl, whisk together the Greek yogurt, lemon juice, olive oil, salt, and black pepper until well combined.
Step 3: Pour the dressing over the cucumber mixture and toss gently to coat all the ingredients evenly.
Step 4: Let the salad sit for 10 minutes to allow the flavors to meld together before serving.

This cucumber and dill salad is a refreshing and nutritious dish, perfect for a low-carb, high-fiber diet. It's quick to prepare and packed with fresh flavors, making it an excellent addition to any meal.

Nutritional Values: Calories 70 | Carb 8 g | Protein 3 g | Fiber 2 g | Fat 3 g | Sugar 4 g

6.9 Avocado and shrimp salad

Preparation Time: 10 min | **Cooking Time:** 10 min | **Servings:** 2

Ingredients:
- Shrimp: 8 oz (peeled and deveined)
- Avocado: 1 large (diced)
- Cherry tomatoes: 1 cup (halved)
- Red onion: 1/4 cup (thinly sliced)
- Cucumber: 1/2 cup (diced)
- Mixed greens: 4 cups
- Olive oil: 2 tbsp
- Lime juice: 2 tbsp
- Garlic: 1 clove (minced)
- Salt: to taste
- Black pepper: to taste

- Fresh cilantro: 2 tbsp (chopped)

Instructions:
Step 1: In a medium skillet, heat 1 tablespoon of olive oil over medium heat. Add the shrimp and cook for about 2-3 minutes on each side until they are pink and opaque. Remove from heat and set aside to cool.
Step 2: In a large bowl, combine the mixed greens, cherry tomatoes, red onion, cucumber, and avocado.
Step 3: In a small bowl, whisk together the remaining olive oil, lime juice, minced garlic, salt, and black pepper to make the dressing.
Step 4: Add the cooked shrimp to the salad bowl and drizzle with the dressing. Toss gently to combine.
Step 5: Garnish with fresh cilantro and serve immediately.

This avocado and shrimp salad is a delightful blend of creamy avocado, succulent shrimp, and crisp vegetables, making it a nutritious and satisfying meal that's quick to prepare and perfect for a low-carb diet.

Nutritional Values: Calories 350 | Carb 15 g | Protein 25 g | Fiber 8 g | Fat 22 g | Sugar 5 g

6.10 Roasted vegetable salad

Preparation Time: 15 min | Cooking Time: 30 min | Servings: 2

Ingredients:
- Bell peppers: 1 large, sliced
- Zucchini: 1 medium, sliced
- Red onion: 1 small, sliced
- Cherry tomatoes: 1 cup, halved
- Olive oil: 2 tablespoons
- Mixed greens: 4 cups
- Feta cheese: 1/4 cup, crumbled
- Balsamic vinegar: 1 tablespoon
- Salt: 1/2 teaspoon
- Black pepper: 1/4 teaspoon
- Fresh basil: 2 tablespoons, chopped

Instructions:
Step 1: Preheat the oven to 425°F (220°C).
Step 2: In a large bowl, toss the bell peppers, zucchini, red onion, and cherry tomatoes with olive oil, salt, and black pepper.
Step 3: Spread the vegetables in a single layer on a baking sheet and roast for 25-30 minutes, or until tender and slightly charred.
Step 4: In a large salad bowl, combine the mixed greens and roasted vegetables.
Step 5: Sprinkle the crumbled feta cheese and fresh basil over the salad.
Step 6: Drizzle with balsamic vinegar and toss gently to combine.

This roasted vegetable salad is a delightful mix of flavors and textures, perfect for a nutritious and satisfying meal. It's low in carbohydrates and high in fiber, making it an excellent choice for a healthy diet.

Nutritional Values: Calories 250 | Carbs 20 g | Protein 6 g | Fiber 6 g | Fat 18 g | Sugar 10 g

6.11 Smoked salmon and arugula salad

Preparation Time: 10 min | Cooking Time: 0 min | Servings: 2

Ingredients:
- Arugula: 4 cups
- Smoked salmon: 4 oz
- Cherry tomatoes: 1 cup, halved
- Red onion: 1/4, thinly sliced
- Avocado: 1, sliced
- Capers: 2 tbsp
- Lemon juice: 2 tbsp
- Olive oil: 2 tbsp
- Dijon mustard: 1 tsp
- Salt: to taste
- Black pepper: to taste

Instructions:
Step 1: In a large bowl, combine the arugula, cherry tomatoes, red onion, and capers.
Step 2: In a small bowl, whisk together the lemon juice, olive oil, Dijon mustard, salt, and black pepper to create the dressing.
Step 3: Drizzle the dressing over the salad and toss gently to combine.
Step 4: Arrange the smoked salmon and avocado slices on top of the salad.
Step 5: Serve immediately and enjoy a fresh, flavorful, and nutritious meal.

This smoked salmon and arugula salad is a delightful blend of flavors and textures, perfect for a quick and healthy meal. It's low in carbohydrates and high in fiber, making it an excellent choice for a balanced diet.

Nutritional Values: Calories 320 | Carb 12 g | Protein 18 g | Fiber 7 g | Fat 24 g | Sugar 3 g

6.12 Watermelon and feta salad

Preparation Time: 15 min | Cooking Time: 0 min | Servings: 2

Ingredients:
- Watermelon: 4 cups, cubed
- Feta cheese: 1/2 cup, crumbled
- Red onion: 1/4 cup, thinly sliced
- Fresh mint leaves: 1/4 cup, chopped
- Fresh basil leaves: 1/4 cup, chopped
- Extra virgin olive oil: 2 tablespoons
- Fresh lime juice: 1 tablespoon

- Salt: to taste
- Black pepper: to taste

Instructions:
Step 1: In a large bowl, combine the cubed watermelon, crumbled feta cheese, thinly sliced red onion, chopped mint leaves, and chopped basil leaves.
Step 2: In a small bowl, whisk together the extra virgin olive oil, fresh lime juice, salt, and black pepper.
Step 3: Drizzle the dressing over the watermelon mixture and gently toss to combine.
Step 4: Serve immediately or refrigerate for up to 1 hour to allow the flavors to meld.

This watermelon and feta salad is a refreshing and vibrant dish, perfect for a light summer meal. It's packed with hydrating watermelon, tangy feta, and fresh herbs, making it both delicious and nutritious.

Nutritional Values: Calories 180 | Carbs 20 g | Protein 5 g | Fiber 2 g | Fat 10 g | Sugar 15 g

6.13 Tuna and white bean salad

Preparation Time: 10 min | Cooking Time: 10 min | Servings: 2

Ingredients:
- Canned tuna: 1 can (5 oz), drained
- White beans: 1 can (15 oz), drained and rinsed
- Cherry tomatoes: 1 cup, halved
- Red onion: 1/4 cup, finely chopped
- Fresh parsley: 1/4 cup, chopped
- Olive oil: 2 tablespoons
- Lemon juice: 2 tablespoons
- Dijon mustard: 1 teaspoon
- Salt: 1/2 teaspoon
- Black pepper: 1/4 teaspoon
- Mixed greens: 2 cups

Instructions:
Step 1: In a large bowl, combine the drained tuna, white beans, cherry tomatoes, red onion, and parsley.
Step 2: In a small bowl, whisk together the olive oil, lemon juice, Dijon mustard, salt, and black pepper until well combined.
Step 3: Pour the dressing over the tuna and bean mixture and toss gently to coat.
Step 4: Divide the mixed greens between two plates and top with the tuna and bean mixture.
Step 5: Serve immediately or chill in the refrigerator for 30 minutes for flavors to meld.

This tuna and white bean salad is a perfect blend of protein and fiber, making it a satisfying and nutritious meal. It's quick to prepare and ideal for a light lunch or dinner.

Nutritional Values: Calories 350 | Carb 30 g | Protein 25 g | Fiber 10 g | Fat 15 g | Sugar 3 g

6.14 Broccoli and almond salad

Preparation Time: 10 min | Cooking Time: 10 min | Servings: 2

Ingredients:
- Broccoli florets: 2 cups
- Sliced almonds: 1/4 cup
- Red onion: 1/4 cup, finely chopped
- Dried cranberries: 1/4 cup
- Feta cheese: 1/4 cup, crumbled
- Olive oil: 2 tablespoons
- Apple cider vinegar: 1 tablespoon
- Dijon mustard: 1 teaspoon
- Honey: 1 teaspoon
- Salt: 1/4 teaspoon
- Black pepper: 1/4 teaspoon

Instructions:
Step 1: Steam the broccoli florets for 5-7 minutes until tender but still crisp. Rinse with cold water to stop the cooking process and drain well.
Step 2: In a large bowl, combine the steamed broccoli, sliced almonds, finely chopped red onion, dried cranberries, and crumbled feta cheese.
Step 3: In a small bowl, whisk together the olive oil, apple cider vinegar, Dijon mustard, honey, salt, and black pepper to make the dressing.
Step 4: Pour the dressing over the broccoli mixture and toss to coat evenly.
Step 5: Serve immediately or refrigerate for up to 2 hours to allow the flavors to meld.

This broccoli and almond salad is a delightful combination of textures and flavors, perfect for a nutritious and satisfying meal. It's quick to prepare and packed with fiber and protein, making it an excellent choice for a healthy diet.

Nutritional Values: Calories 220 | Carb 18 g | Protein 7 g | Fiber 5 g | Fat 14 g | Sugar 8 g

6.15 Pear and blue cheese salad

Preparation Time: 10 min | Cooking Time: 0 min | Servings: 2

Ingredients:
- Mixed greens: 4 cups
- Pear: 1, thinly sliced
- Blue cheese: 1/4 cup, crumbled
- Walnuts: 1/4 cup, toasted
- Red onion: 1/4 cup, thinly sliced
- Balsamic vinaigrette: 2 tablespoons

Instructions:

Step 1: In a large salad bowl, combine the mixed greens, thinly sliced pear, crumbled blue cheese, toasted walnuts, and thinly sliced red onion.
Step 2: Drizzle the balsamic vinaigrette over the salad.
Step 3: Toss gently to combine all ingredients evenly.
Step 4: Serve immediately and enjoy the fresh, vibrant flavors.

This pear and blue cheese salad is a delightful combination of sweet and savory flavors, perfect for a quick and nutritious meal. It's low in carbohydrates and high in fiber, making it a great addition to a healthy diet.

Nutritional Values: Calories 250 | Carb 20 g | Protein 6 g | Fiber 4 g | Fat 18 g | Sugar 12 g

6.16 Buffalo chicken salad

Preparation Time: 15 min | Cooking Time: 15 min | Servings: 2

Ingredients:
- Chicken breast: 8 oz, boneless and skinless
- Olive oil: 1 tbsp
- Buffalo sauce: 1/4 cup
- Romaine lettuce: 4 cups, chopped
- Cherry tomatoes: 1 cup, halved
- Red onion: 1/4 cup, thinly sliced
- Celery: 1/2 cup, sliced
- Blue cheese crumbles: 1/4 cup
- Ranch dressing: 1/4 cup
- Salt: to taste
- Black pepper: to taste

Instructions:
Step 1: Preheat a grill or skillet over medium-high heat. Season the chicken breast with salt and black pepper.
Step 2: Drizzle olive oil over the chicken and grill or cook in the skillet for about 6-7 minutes on each side, or until fully cooked. Remove from heat and let rest for 5 minutes.
Step 3: Slice the cooked chicken into strips and toss with buffalo sauce until well-coated.
Step 4: In a large bowl, combine romaine lettuce, cherry tomatoes, red onion, and celery.
Step 5: Top the salad with buffalo chicken strips and sprinkle blue cheese crumbles over the top.
Step 6: Drizzle ranch dressing over the salad and toss gently to combine all ingredients.
Step 7: Serve immediately and enjoy the bold flavors of this delicious buffalo chicken salad.

This buffalo chicken salad is a perfect blend of spicy and tangy flavors, combined with fresh vegetables and creamy blue cheese. It's a quick and nutritious meal that fits perfectly into a low-carb, high-fiber diet.

Nutritional Values: Calories 400 | Carb 12 g | Protein 35 g | Fiber 4 g | Fat 25 g | Sugar 5 g

6.17 Greek salad with grilled lamb

Preparation Time: 15 min | Cooking Time: 20 min | Servings: 2

Ingredients:
- Boneless lamb loin chops: 8 oz
- Olive oil: 2 tbsp
- Lemon juice: 1 tbsp
- Garlic: 2 cloves, minced
- Dried oregano: 1 tsp
- Salt: 1/2 tsp
- Black pepper: 1/4 tsp
- Romaine lettuce: 4 cups, chopped
- Cherry tomatoes: 1 cup, halved
- Cucumber: 1, sliced
- Red onion: 1/4, thinly sliced
- Kalamata olives: 1/4 cup, pitted and halved
- Feta cheese: 1/4 cup, crumbled
- Red wine vinegar: 1 tbsp
- Dijon mustard: 1 tsp

Instructions:
Step 1: In a small bowl, mix olive oil, lemon juice, minced garlic, dried oregano, salt, and black pepper. Rub the mixture onto the lamb chops and let them marinate for at least 10 minutes.
Step 2: Preheat the grill to medium-high heat. Grill the lamb chops for about 4-5 minutes on each side or until they reach your desired level of doneness. Remove from the grill and let them rest for a few minutes before slicing.
Step 3: In a large bowl, combine chopped romaine lettuce, cherry tomatoes, cucumber slices, red onion, and Kalamata olives.
Step 4: In a small bowl, whisk together red wine vinegar and Dijon mustard. Drizzle over the salad and toss to combine.
Step 5: Top the salad with crumbled feta cheese and sliced grilled lamb.

This Greek salad with grilled lamb is a perfect blend of fresh vegetables and savory protein, making it a delicious and nutritious meal that's quick to prepare and full of flavor.

Nutritional Values: Calories 450 | Carbs 12 g | Protein 35 g | Fiber 4 g | Fat 30 g | Sugar 6 g

6.18 Carrot and raisin salad

Preparation Time: 10 min | Cooking Time: 0 min | Servings: 2

Ingredients:
- Carrots: 2 cups, shredded
- Raisins: 1/2 cup
- Greek yogurt: 1/4 cup

- Honey: 1 tbsp
- Lemon juice: 1 tbsp
- Salt: 1/4 tsp
- Black pepper: 1/8 tsp
- Fresh parsley: 1 tbsp, chopped (optional)

Instructions:
Step 1: In a large bowl, combine the shredded carrots and raisins.
Step 2: In a small bowl, whisk together the Greek yogurt, honey, lemon juice, salt, and black pepper until well combined.
Step 3: Pour the dressing over the carrot and raisin mixture and toss until everything is evenly coated.
Step 4: Garnish with chopped fresh parsley if desired.
Step 5: Chill in the refrigerator for at least 10 minutes before serving to allow the flavors to meld.

This carrot and raisin salad is a delightful blend of sweet and tangy flavors, perfect for a quick and nutritious side dish. It's high in fiber and low in carbs, making it an excellent addition to a healthy diet.

Nutritional Values: Calories 150 | Carb 30 g | Protein 4 g | Fiber 4 g | Fat 2 g | Sugar 20 g

SCAN THE QR CODE
TO ACCESS
YOUR EXCLUSIVE BONUS
info@retoteufel.com

7. Soothing and hearty soups
7.1 Classic chicken noodle soup

Preparation Time: 10 min | Cooking Time: 25 min | Servings: 2

Ingredients:
- Chicken breast, boneless and skinless: 1/2 lb
- Olive oil: 1 tbsp
- Carrot, diced: 1 medium
- Celery stalk, diced: 1
- Onion, diced: 1/2 medium
- Garlic, minced: 2 cloves
- Low-sodium chicken broth: 4 cups
- Egg noodles: 1 cup
- Fresh parsley, chopped: 2 tbsp
- Salt: to taste
- Black pepper: to taste

Instructions:
Step 1: Heat the olive oil in a large pot over medium heat. Add the diced onion, carrot, and celery. Sauté for about 5 minutes until the vegetables are softened.
Step 2: Add the minced garlic and cook for an additional 1 minute until fragrant.
Step 3: Pour in the low-sodium chicken broth and bring to a boil.
Step 4: Add the chicken breast to the pot. Reduce the heat to a simmer and cook for about 15 minutes, or until the chicken is cooked through.
Step 5: Remove the chicken from the pot and shred it using two forks. Return the shredded chicken to the pot.
Step 6: Add the egg noodles to the pot and cook according to the package instructions, usually about 6-8 minutes.
Step 7: Season the soup with salt and black pepper to taste. Stir in the chopped fresh parsley before serving.

This classic chicken noodle soup is not only comforting and delicious but also diabetic-friendly, making it a perfect addition to your collection of hearty soups.

Nutritional Values: Calories 250 | Carbs 25 g | Protein 20 g | Fiber 3 g | Fat 8 g | Sugar 4 g

7.2 Creamy tomato basil soup

Preparation Time: 10 min | Cooking Time: 20 min | Servings: 2

Ingredients:
- Olive oil: 1 tbsp
- Onion: 1 small, finely chopped
- Garlic: 2 cloves, minced
- Canned crushed tomatoes: 1 can (14.5 oz)
- Vegetable broth: 1 cup
- Heavy cream: 1/4 cup
- Fresh basil leaves: 1/4 cup, chopped
- Salt: 1/2 tsp
- Black pepper: 1/4 tsp
- Parmesan cheese: 2 tbsp, grated (optional)

Instructions:
Step 1: Heat the olive oil in a large pot over medium heat. Add the chopped onion and cook until softened, about 5 minutes.
Step 2: Add the minced garlic and cook for another minute, until fragrant.
Step 3: Pour in the canned crushed tomatoes and vegetable broth. Stir to combine.
Step 4: Bring the mixture to a simmer and cook for 10 minutes, allowing the flavors to meld.
Step 5: Remove the pot from heat and use an immersion blender to puree the soup until smooth. Alternatively, transfer the soup to a blender in batches and blend until smooth, then return to the pot.
Step 6: Stir in the heavy cream and chopped basil leaves. Season with salt and black pepper to taste.
Step 7: Return the pot to low heat and cook for an additional 5 minutes, stirring occasionally.
Step 8: Serve hot, garnished with grated Parmesan cheese if desired.

This creamy tomato basil soup is a perfect blend of comfort and nutrition, making it an ideal choice for a diabetic-friendly meal. It's quick to prepare and packed with fresh flavors.

Nutritional Values: Calories 180 | Carb 15 g | Protein 3 g | Fiber 3 g | Fat 12 g | Sugar 9 g

7.3 Lentil and spinach soup

Preparation Time: 15 min | Cooking Time: 30 min | Servings: 2

Ingredients:
- Olive oil: 1 tablespoon
- Onion: 1 small, diced
- Garlic: 2 cloves, minced
- Carrot: 1 medium, diced

- Celery: 1 stalk, diced
- Dried lentils: 1/2 cup, rinsed
- Vegetable broth: 4 cups, low-sodium
- Canned diced tomatoes: 1/2 cup, with juice
- Ground cumin: 1 teaspoon
- Ground coriander: 1/2 teaspoon
- Fresh spinach: 2 cups, roughly chopped
- Salt: to taste
- Black pepper: to taste
- Lemon juice: 1 tablespoon (optional)

Instructions:
Step 1: Heat the olive oil in a large pot over medium heat. Add the diced onion, garlic, carrot, and celery. Sauté for about 5 minutes, until the vegetables are softened.
Step 2: Stir in the lentils, vegetable broth, diced tomatoes, cumin, and coriander. Bring the mixture to a boil, then reduce the heat and let it simmer for about 25 minutes, or until the lentils are tender.
Step 3: Add the chopped spinach to the pot and cook for an additional 5 minutes, until the spinach is wilted. Season with salt and black pepper to taste.
Step 4: If desired, stir in the lemon juice just before serving to add a fresh, tangy flavor.

This lentil and spinach soup is not only delicious and comforting but also packed with nutrients. It's a perfect diabetic-friendly option, rich in fiber and low-glycemic ingredients.

Nutritional Values: Calories 220 | Carb 35 g | Protein 12 g | Fiber 14 g | Fat 6 g | Sugar 6 g

7.4 Beef and barley soup

Preparation Time: 15 min | Cooking Time: 1 hr 15 min | Servings: 2

Ingredients:
- Olive oil: 1 tablespoon
- Lean beef stew meat, cubed: 1/2 pound
- Onion, chopped: 1 small
- Carrots, diced: 2 medium
- Celery stalks, diced: 2
- Garlic cloves, minced: 2
- Low-sodium beef broth: 4 cups
- Water: 1 cup
- Pearl barley: 1/4 cup
- Dried thyme: 1/2 teaspoon
- Dried rosemary: 1/2 teaspoon
- Bay leaf: 1
- Salt: to taste
- Black pepper: to taste
- Fresh parsley, chopped: 2 tablespoons

Instructions:
Step 1: Heat the olive oil in a large pot over medium-high heat. Add the beef and cook until browned on all sides. Remove the beef and set aside.
Step 2: In the same pot, add the onion, carrots, and celery. Cook until the vegetables are softened, about 5 minutes. Add the garlic and cook for another minute.
Step 3: Return the beef to the pot. Add the beef broth, water, pearl barley, thyme, rosemary, and bay leaf. Bring to a boil, then reduce the heat to low and simmer for 1 hour, or until the barley is tender.
Step 4: Season with salt and black pepper to taste. Remove the bay leaf.
Step 5: Serve hot, garnished with fresh parsley.

This beef and barley soup is both hearty and nutritious, perfect for a comforting meal. The lean beef and barley provide a good source of protein and fiber, making it a great option for a diabetic-friendly diet.

Nutritional Values: Calories 350 | Carb 35 g | Protein 28 g | Fiber 8 g | Fat 10 g | Sugar 5 g

7.5 Butternut squash and ginger soup

Preparation Time: 15 min | Cooking Time: 30 min | Servings: 2

Ingredients:
- Butternut squash: 1 small (about 1.5 lbs), peeled, seeded, and cubed
- Olive oil: 1 tablespoon
- Onion: 1 small, chopped
- Fresh ginger: 1 tablespoon, grated
- Garlic: 2 cloves, minced
- Vegetable broth: 2 cups, low-sodium
- Coconut milk: 1/2 cup, light
- Salt: 1/2 teaspoon
- Black pepper: 1/4 teaspoon
- Ground cinnamon: 1/4 teaspoon
- Fresh cilantro: for garnish (optional)

Instructions:
Step 1: In a large pot, heat the olive oil over medium heat. Add the chopped onion and cook until softened, about 5 minutes.
Step 2: Add the grated ginger and minced garlic to the pot, cooking for an additional 2 minutes until fragrant.
Step 3: Add the cubed butternut squash to the pot, stirring to combine with the onion, ginger, and garlic mixture.
Step 4: Pour in the vegetable broth and bring the mixture to a boil. Reduce the heat to low, cover, and simmer for 20 minutes, or until the squash is tender.
Step 5: Remove the pot from heat and use an immersion blender to puree the soup until smooth. Alternatively, transfer the soup in batches to a blender and puree until smooth, then return to the pot.
Step 6: Stir in the light coconut milk, salt, black pepper, and ground cinnamon. Adjust seasoning to taste.
Step 7: Reheat the soup over low heat if necessary. Serve hot, garnished with fresh cilantro if desired.

This butternut squash and ginger soup is a perfect blend of sweet and spicy flavors, making it both comforting and nutritious. It's quick to prepare and ideal for a diabetic-friendly diet.

Nutritional Values: Calories 180 | Carbs 30 g | Protein 3 g | Fiber 5 g | Fat 7 g | Sugar 6 g

7.6 Turkey and vegetable soup

Preparation Time: 15 min | Cooking Time: 30 min | Servings: 2

Ingredients:
- Olive oil: 1 tablespoon
- Onion: 1 small, chopped
- Garlic: 2 cloves, minced
- Carrots: 2 medium, sliced
- Celery: 2 stalks, sliced
- Zucchini: 1 medium, diced
- Turkey breast: 8 ounces, cooked and shredded
- Low-sodium chicken broth: 4 cups
- Diced tomatoes: 1 cup, no salt added
- Fresh thyme: 1 teaspoon, chopped
- Fresh parsley: 1 tablespoon, chopped
- Salt: 1/2 teaspoon
- Black pepper: 1/4 teaspoon

Instructions:
Step 1: Heat the olive oil in a large pot over medium heat. Add the chopped onion and minced garlic, and sauté until the onion is translucent, about 3-4 minutes.
Step 2: Add the sliced carrots and celery to the pot and cook for another 5 minutes, stirring occasionally.
Step 3: Stir in the diced zucchini and cook for an additional 3 minutes.
Step 4: Add the cooked and shredded turkey breast to the pot, followed by the low-sodium chicken broth and diced tomatoes. Bring the mixture to a boil.
Step 5: Reduce the heat to low and let the soup simmer for 15 minutes, allowing the flavors to meld together.
Step 6: Stir in the fresh thyme and parsley, and season with salt and black pepper. Cook for another 2 minutes.
Step 7: Serve the soup hot, garnished with additional fresh parsley if desired.

This turkey and vegetable soup is a perfect blend of lean protein and nutrient-rich vegetables, making it a comforting and diabetic-friendly option for a hearty meal.

Nutritional Values: Calories 250 | Carb 20 g | Protein 30 g | Fiber 5 g | Fat 7 g | Sugar 6 g

7.7 Cauliflower and leek soup

Preparation Time: 10 min | Cooking Time: 20 min | Servings: 2

Ingredients:
- Cauliflower: 1 small head, chopped

- Leeks: 2, white and light green parts only, sliced
- Olive oil: 1 tablespoon
- Garlic: 2 cloves, minced
- Low-sodium vegetable broth: 3 cups
- Unsweetened almond milk: 1/2 cup
- Salt: 1/2 teaspoon
- Black pepper: 1/4 teaspoon
- Fresh thyme: 1 teaspoon, chopped (optional)
- Fresh parsley: for garnish (optional)

Instructions:
Step 1: Heat the olive oil in a large pot over medium heat. Add the leeks and garlic, and sauté until softened, about 5 minutes.
Step 2: Add the chopped cauliflower to the pot and cook for another 5 minutes, stirring occasionally.
Step 3: Pour in the vegetable broth, bring to a boil, then reduce the heat and let it simmer for 15 minutes, or until the cauliflower is tender.
Step 4: Remove the pot from the heat and use an immersion blender to puree the soup until smooth. Alternatively, transfer the soup to a blender in batches and blend until smooth.
Step 5: Stir in the almond milk, salt, and black pepper. Reheat the soup gently if necessary.
Step 6: Serve hot, garnished with fresh thyme and parsley if desired.

This cauliflower and leek soup is a creamy, comforting dish that's perfect for a cozy meal. It's low in carbs and packed with nutrients, making it an excellent choice for a diabetic-friendly diet.

Nutritional Values: Calories 130 | Carb 18 g | Protein 4 g | Fiber 5 g | Fat 6 g | Sugar 5 g

7.8 Miso soup with tofu and seaweed

Preparation Time: 10 min | Cooking Time: 10 min | Servings: 2

Ingredients:
- Water: 3 cups
- White miso paste: 2 tablespoons
- Firm tofu: 4 ounces, cubed
- Dried seaweed (wakame): 1 tablespoon
- Green onions: 2, thinly sliced
- Soy sauce: 1 teaspoon (optional)
- Sesame oil: 1/2 teaspoon (optional)

Instructions:
Step 1: In a medium pot, bring the water to a gentle simmer over medium heat.
Step 2: Add the miso paste to the pot and whisk until fully dissolved.
Step 3: Add the cubed tofu and dried seaweed to the pot, and simmer for 5 minutes until the seaweed is rehydrated and the tofu is heated through.
Step 4: Stir in the green onions and soy sauce (if using), and simmer for another 2 minutes.
Step 5: Remove from heat, drizzle with sesame oil (if using), and serve hot.

This miso soup is a quick and easy recipe that provides a comforting and nutritious meal, perfect for a diabetic-friendly diet. The combination of tofu and seaweed offers a good source of protein and essential minerals.

Nutritional Values: Calories 70 | Carb 6 g | Protein 6 g | Fiber 1 g | Fat 3 g | Sugar 1 g

7.9 Minestrone with whole grain pasta

Preparation Time: 15 min | Cooking Time: 30 min | Servings: 2

Ingredients:
- Olive oil: 1 tablespoon
- Onion: 1 small, diced
- Carrot: 1 medium, diced
- Celery: 1 stalk, diced
- Garlic: 2 cloves, minced
- Zucchini: 1 small, diced
- Green beans: 1/2 cup, chopped
- Diced tomatoes: 1 can (14.5 oz)
- Vegetable broth: 3 cups, low-sodium
- Cannellini beans: 1/2 cup, drained and rinsed
- Whole grain pasta: 1/2 cup, uncooked
- Fresh spinach: 1 cup, chopped
- Dried oregano: 1/2 teaspoon
- Dried basil: 1/2 teaspoon
- Salt: to taste
- Black pepper: to taste
- Parmesan cheese: 2 tablespoons, grated (optional)

Instructions:
Step 1: Heat the olive oil in a large pot over medium heat. Add the diced onion, carrot, and celery. Sauté for about 5 minutes until the vegetables are softened.
Step 2: Add the minced garlic, diced zucchini, and chopped green beans. Cook for an additional 3 minutes.
Step 3: Stir in the canned diced tomatoes, vegetable broth, and cannellini beans. Bring the mixture to a boil.
Step 4: Once boiling, add the whole grain pasta. Reduce the heat and let it simmer for about 10 minutes or until the pasta is al dente.
Step 5: Add the chopped spinach, dried oregano, and dried basil. Season with salt and black pepper to taste. Simmer for another 5 minutes.
Step 6: Serve hot, garnished with grated Parmesan cheese if desired.

This minestrone with whole grain pasta is a hearty and nutritious soup, perfect for a comforting meal. It's packed with vegetables and whole grains, making it a great option for a diabetic-friendly diet.

Nutritional Values: Calories 250 | Carbs 45 g | Protein 10 g | Fiber 8 g | Fat 6 g | Sugar 8 g

7.10 Spicy black bean soup

Preparation Time: 10 min | Cooking Time: 30 min | Servings: 2

Ingredients:
- Black beans (canned, drained and rinsed): 1 can (15 oz)
- Olive oil: 1 tbsp
- Onion (chopped): 1 small
- Garlic (minced): 2 cloves
- Red bell pepper (chopped): 1/2
- Jalapeño pepper (seeded and minced): 1
- Vegetable broth (low-sodium): 2 cups
- Cumin (ground): 1 tsp
- Smoked paprika: 1/2 tsp
- Chili powder: 1/2 tsp
- Salt: 1/4 tsp
- Black pepper: 1/4 tsp
- Lime juice: 1 tbsp
- Fresh cilantro (chopped): 2 tbsp (optional for garnish)
- Greek yogurt (non-fat): 2 tbsp (optional for garnish)

Instructions:
Step 1: Heat the olive oil in a large pot over medium heat. Add the chopped onion and cook until softened, about 5 minutes.
Step 2: Add the minced garlic, chopped red bell pepper, and minced jalapeño pepper. Cook for another 3-4 minutes until the vegetables are tender.
Step 3: Stir in the ground cumin, smoked paprika, and chili powder. Cook for 1 minute to toast the spices.
Step 4: Add the black beans and vegetable broth to the pot. Bring to a boil, then reduce the heat and simmer for 15 minutes.
Step 5: Use an immersion blender to partially blend the soup, leaving some chunks for texture. Alternatively, transfer half of the soup to a blender, blend until smooth, and return to the pot.
Step 6: Stir in the lime juice, salt, and black pepper. Adjust seasoning to taste.
Step 7: Serve hot, garnished with fresh cilantro and a dollop of Greek yogurt if desired.

This spicy black bean soup is a perfect blend of heat and heartiness, making it a comforting and nutritious option for those following a diabetic-friendly diet. It's quick to prepare and packed with flavor!

Nutritional Values: Calories 220 | Carbs 36 g | Protein 11 g | Fiber 12 g | Fat 5 g | Sugar 3 g

7.11 Pumpkin and sage soup

Preparation Time: 15 min | Cooking Time: 30 min | Servings: 2

Ingredients:
- Pumpkin puree: 2 cups

- Vegetable broth: 2 cups
- Onion: 1 small, finely chopped
- Garlic: 2 cloves, minced
- Fresh sage: 6 leaves, finely chopped
- Olive oil: 1 tablespoon
- Salt: 1/2 teaspoon
- Black pepper: 1/4 teaspoon
- Ground nutmeg: 1/8 teaspoon
- Heavy cream: 1/4 cup (optional for garnish)
- Pumpkin seeds: 2 tablespoons (optional for garnish)

Instructions:
Step 1: Heat the olive oil in a large pot over medium heat. Add the chopped onion and garlic, and sauté until the onion is translucent, about 5 minutes.
Step 2: Add the pumpkin puree, vegetable broth, chopped sage, salt, black pepper, and ground nutmeg. Stir to combine.
Step 3: Bring the mixture to a boil, then reduce the heat and let it simmer for 20 minutes, stirring occasionally.
Step 4: Use an immersion blender to puree the soup until smooth. Alternatively, transfer the soup in batches to a blender and blend until smooth, then return it to the pot.
Step 5: Taste and adjust seasoning if necessary. If using, drizzle the heavy cream on top and sprinkle with pumpkin seeds before serving.

This pumpkin and sage soup is a perfect blend of comforting flavors and nutritious ingredients, making it an ideal choice for a diabetic-friendly diet. It's quick to prepare and offers a soothing warmth that's perfect for any season.

Nutritional Values: Calories 150 | Carbs 20 g | Protein 3 g | Fiber 4 g | Fat 7 g | Sugar 6 g

7.12 Chicken tortilla soup

Preparation Time: 15 min | Cooking Time: 30 min | Servings: 2

Ingredients:
- Olive oil: 1 tablespoon
- Onion: 1/2 medium, diced
- Garlic: 2 cloves, minced
- Chicken breast: 1, boneless and skinless, diced
- Chicken broth: 3 cups, low-sodium
- Diced tomatoes: 1 can (14.5 oz), no salt added
- Black beans: 1/2 cup, cooked and drained
- Corn kernels: 1/2 cup, fresh or frozen
- Green bell pepper: 1/2 medium, diced
- Ground cumin: 1 teaspoon
- Chili powder: 1 teaspoon
- Salt: 1/2 teaspoon
- Black pepper: 1/4 teaspoon

- Fresh cilantro: 2 tablespoons, chopped
- Lime juice: 1 tablespoon
- Tortilla chips: 1/2 cup, crushed
- Avocado: 1/2, sliced (optional for garnish)

Instructions:
Step 1: Heat olive oil in a large pot over medium heat. Add diced onion and minced garlic, sauté until fragrant and translucent, about 3-4 minutes.
Step 2: Add diced chicken breast to the pot and cook until browned on all sides, about 5-6 minutes.
Step 3: Pour in the chicken broth and diced tomatoes, then add black beans, corn kernels, and green bell pepper. Stir to combine.
Step 4: Season the soup with ground cumin, chili powder, salt, and black pepper. Bring the mixture to a boil, then reduce heat and let it simmer for 20 minutes.
Step 5: Stir in fresh cilantro and lime juice. Adjust seasoning if necessary.
Step 6: Ladle the soup into bowls and top with crushed tortilla chips and avocado slices if desired.

This chicken tortilla soup is a perfect blend of flavors and textures, offering a comforting and nutritious meal that's quick to prepare. It's diabetic-friendly and packed with protein and fiber, making it a hearty option for any day.

Nutritional Values: Calories 320 | Carb 35 g | Protein 25 g | Fiber 8 g | Fat 10 g | Sugar 6 g

7.13 White bean and kale soup

Preparation Time: 15 min | Cooking Time: 30 min | Servings: 2

Ingredients:
- Olive oil: 1 tablespoon
- Yellow onion, diced: 1/2 medium
- Garlic cloves, minced: 2
- Carrots, diced: 1 medium
- Celery stalks, diced: 1
- Vegetable broth: 3 cups
- Canned white beans, drained and rinsed: 1 can (15 ounces)
- Fresh kale, chopped: 2 cups
- Dried thyme: 1/2 teaspoon
- Dried rosemary: 1/2 teaspoon
- Salt: 1/2 teaspoon
- Black pepper: 1/4 teaspoon
- Lemon juice: 1 tablespoon

Instructions:
Step 1: Heat the olive oil in a large pot over medium heat. Add the diced onion and sauté for 5 minutes until translucent.
Step 2: Add the minced garlic, diced carrots, and diced celery to the pot. Cook for another 5 minutes, stirring occasionally.

Step 3: Pour in the vegetable broth and bring to a boil. Reduce the heat to low and simmer for 10 minutes.
Step 4: Add the drained and rinsed white beans, chopped kale, dried thyme, dried rosemary, salt, and black pepper. Stir well and simmer for another 10 minutes until the kale is tender.
Step 5: Stir in the lemon juice and adjust seasoning if necessary. Serve hot.

This white bean and kale soup is not only delicious but also packed with nutrients. It's a perfect choice for a comforting meal that aligns with diabetic-friendly guidelines.

Nutritional Values: Calories 220 | Carbs 36 g | Protein 10 g | Fiber 10 g | Fat 5 g | Sugar 4 g

7.14 Carrot and coriander soup

Preparation Time: 10 min | Cooking Time: 20 min | Servings: 2

Ingredients:
- Carrots: 2 cups, chopped
- Onion: 1 small, chopped
- Garlic: 2 cloves, minced
- Fresh coriander: 1/4 cup, chopped
- Vegetable broth: 2 cups, low-sodium
- Olive oil: 1 tablespoon
- Ground coriander: 1 teaspoon
- Salt: to taste
- Black pepper: to taste

Instructions:
Step 1: Heat the olive oil in a large pot over medium heat. Add the chopped onion and garlic, and sauté until softened, about 3-4 minutes.
Step 2: Add the chopped carrots and ground coriander to the pot, stirring well to combine. Cook for another 5 minutes.
Step 3: Pour in the vegetable broth and bring the mixture to a boil. Reduce the heat and let it simmer for 15 minutes, or until the carrots are tender.
Step 4: Remove the pot from the heat and let it cool slightly. Use an immersion blender to puree the soup until smooth. Alternatively, transfer the soup in batches to a blender and blend until smooth.
Step 5: Stir in the fresh coriander and season with salt and black pepper to taste. Reheat the soup if necessary before serving.

This carrot and coriander soup is not only delicious and comforting but also diabetic-friendly, thanks to its low-glycemic ingredients. It's quick to prepare and perfect for a cozy meal.

Nutritional Values: Calories 120 | Carbs 20 g | Protein 2 g | Fiber 5 g | Fat 5 g | Sugar 8 g

7.15 Pea and mint soup

Preparation Time: 10 min | Cooking Time: 15 min | Servings: 2

Ingredients:
- Olive oil: 1 tbsp
- Onion: 1 small, finely chopped
- Garlic: 1 clove, minced
- Frozen peas: 2 cups
- Vegetable broth: 2 cups, low-sodium
- Fresh mint leaves: 1/4 cup, chopped
- Salt: to taste
- Black pepper: to taste
- Greek yogurt: 2 tbsp (optional, for garnish)

Instructions:
Step 1: Heat the olive oil in a medium saucepan over medium heat. Add the chopped onion and garlic, and sauté until softened, about 3-4 minutes.
Step 2: Add the frozen peas and vegetable broth to the saucepan. Bring to a boil, then reduce the heat and simmer for 5-7 minutes, until the peas are tender.
Step 3: Remove the saucepan from the heat and stir in the chopped mint leaves. Season with salt and black pepper to taste.
Step 4: Use an immersion blender to puree the soup until smooth. Alternatively, transfer the soup to a blender and blend until smooth, then return to the saucepan.
Step 5: Reheat the soup gently if needed. Serve hot, garnished with a dollop of Greek yogurt if desired.

This pea and mint soup is a quick and easy recipe that is both refreshing and comforting. It's perfect for a diabetic-friendly diet, using low-glycemic ingredients and providing a good balance of nutrients.

Nutritional Values: Calories 150 | Carbs 22 g | Protein 6 g | Fiber 7 g | Fat 5 g | Sugar 6 g

7.16 Mushroom and thyme soup

Preparation Time: 15 min | Cooking Time: 30 min | Servings: 2

Ingredients:
- Olive oil: 1 tablespoon
- Onion: 1 small, finely chopped
- Garlic: 2 cloves, minced
- Fresh thyme: 1 tablespoon, chopped
- Button mushrooms: 10 ounces, sliced
- Low-sodium vegetable broth: 2 cups
- Unsweetened almond milk: 1 cup
- Salt: 1/2 teaspoon
- Black pepper: 1/4 teaspoon
- Fresh parsley: 1 tablespoon, chopped (for garnish)

Instructions:
Step 1: Heat the olive oil in a large pot over medium heat. Add the finely chopped onion and sauté for 5 minutes

until softened.
Step 2: Add the minced garlic and chopped thyme, and cook for another 2 minutes until fragrant.
Step 3: Add the sliced mushrooms to the pot and cook for 10 minutes, stirring occasionally, until they release their juices and become tender.
Step 4: Pour in the low-sodium vegetable broth and bring to a boil. Reduce the heat and simmer for 10 minutes.
Step 5: Stir in the unsweetened almond milk, salt, and black pepper. Simmer for an additional 5 minutes.
Step 6: Use an immersion blender to blend the soup until smooth, or transfer to a blender in batches if necessary.
Step 7: Ladle the soup into bowls and garnish with chopped fresh parsley before serving.

This mushroom and thyme soup is a comforting and nutritious option, perfect for a diabetic-friendly diet. It's quick to prepare and full of rich, earthy flavors.

Nutritional Values: Calories 120 | Carb 12 g | Protein 4 g | Fiber 3 g | Fat 7 g | Sugar 3 g

7.17 Asian chicken and ginger broth

Preparation Time: 15 min | Cooking Time: 30 min | Servings: 2

Ingredients:
- Chicken breast: 1 (about 8 oz), skinless and boneless
- Fresh ginger: 2 inches, peeled and thinly sliced
- Garlic: 2 cloves, minced
- Low-sodium chicken broth: 4 cups
- Soy sauce: 1 tbsp
- Fish sauce: 1 tsp
- Baby bok choy: 2 heads, halved
- Carrot: 1, julienned
- Green onions: 2, thinly sliced
- Fresh cilantro: 2 tbsp, chopped
- Lime: 1, cut into wedges
- Salt: to taste
- Black pepper: to taste

Instructions:
Step 1: In a large pot, bring the chicken broth to a boil. Add the ginger and garlic, then reduce the heat and let it simmer for 10 minutes to infuse the flavors.
Step 2: Add the chicken breast to the pot and cook for about 15 minutes, or until the chicken is cooked through. Remove the chicken and set it aside to cool slightly.
Step 3: Add the soy sauce and fish sauce to the broth. Taste and adjust seasoning with salt and pepper as needed.
Step 4: Shred the cooked chicken into bite-sized pieces and return it to the pot. Add the baby bok choy and carrots, and cook for another 5 minutes until the vegetables are tender.
Step 5: Ladle the soup into bowls and garnish with green onions and cilantro. Serve with lime wedges on the side for an extra burst of flavor.

This Asian chicken and ginger broth is a perfect blend of soothing and hearty, making it an ideal choice for a comforting meal. It's packed with protein and low-glycemic vegetables, adhering to the dietary focus of the book.

Nutritional Values: Calories 220 | Carb 10 g | Protein 30 g | Fiber 2 g | Fat 5 g | Sugar 4 g

7.18 Split pea and ham soup

Preparation Time: 15 min | Cooking Time: 1 hr 30 min | Servings: 2

Ingredients:
- Split peas: 1/2 cup, dried
- Ham: 4 oz, diced
- Onion: 1/2 medium, chopped
- Carrot: 1 medium, chopped
- Celery: 1 stalk, chopped
- Garlic: 1 clove, minced
- Olive oil: 1 tbsp
- Chicken broth: 3 cups, low-sodium
- Bay leaf: 1
- Thyme: 1/2 tsp, dried
- Black pepper: 1/4 tsp
- Salt: to taste
- Water: 1 cup

Instructions:
Step 1: Rinse the split peas under cold water and set aside.
Step 2: In a large pot, heat the olive oil over medium heat. Add the onion, carrot, celery, and garlic. Sauté until the vegetables are softened, about 5 minutes.
Step 3: Add the diced ham to the pot and cook for an additional 2 minutes.
Step 4: Add the rinsed split peas, chicken broth, water, bay leaf, thyme, and black pepper to the pot. Stir to combine.
Step 5: Bring the mixture to a boil, then reduce the heat to low. Cover and simmer for 1 hour, stirring occasionally.
Step 6: After 1 hour, check the consistency of the soup. If it is too thick, add a little more water. Continue to simmer for an additional 30 minutes, or until the peas are tender and the soup has thickened.
Step 7: Remove the bay leaf and season with salt to taste before serving.

This split pea and ham soup is a comforting and nutritious option, perfect for a diabetic-friendly diet. It's packed with protein and fiber, making it both hearty and satisfying.

Nutritional Values: Calories 280 | Carb 40 g | Protein 20 g | Fiber 16 g | Fat 6 g | Sugar 6 g

8. Snacks for energy and health

8.1 Almond and pumpkin seed mix

Preparation Time: 5 min | **Cooking Time:** 0 min | **Servings:** 2

Ingredients:
- Almonds: 1/2 cup
- Pumpkin seeds: 1/2 cup
- Dried cranberries: 1/4 cup
- Dark chocolate chips: 2 tbsp
- Sea salt: a pinch (optional)

Instructions:
Step 1: In a medium bowl, combine the almonds, pumpkin seeds, dried cranberries, and dark chocolate chips.
Step 2: Mix well to ensure an even distribution of all ingredients.
Step 3: Optionally, add a pinch of sea salt and mix again.
Step 4: Divide the mixture into two equal portions and serve immediately or store in an airtight container for later use.

This almond and pumpkin seed mix is a perfect snack for maintaining energy levels throughout the day. It's quick to prepare, rich in nutrients, and ideal for a healthy diet.

Nutritional Values: Calories 250 | Carbs 22 g | Protein 8 g | Fiber 5 g | Fat 18 g | Sugar 10 g

8.2 Chia and berry yogurt parfait

Preparation Time: 10 min | **Cooking Time:** 0 min | **Servings:** 2

Ingredients:
- Greek yogurt: 1 cup
- Chia seeds: 2 tablespoons
- Fresh mixed berries (strawberries, blueberries, raspberries): 1 cup
- Honey: 2 teaspoons
- Vanilla extract: 1/2 teaspoon

- Almonds (sliced): 2 tablespoons
- Mint leaves (optional, for garnish): a few leaves

Instructions:
Step 1: In a medium bowl, mix the Greek yogurt with the chia seeds, honey, and vanilla extract. Stir well to combine.
Step 2: Divide half of the yogurt mixture evenly between two serving glasses.
Step 3: Layer half of the mixed berries on top of the yogurt mixture in each glass.
Step 4: Add the remaining yogurt mixture on top of the berry layer in each glass.
Step 5: Top with the remaining mixed berries and sprinkle with sliced almonds.
Step 6: Garnish with mint leaves if desired.

A delightful and nutritious snack, this chia and berry yogurt parfait is quick to prepare and perfect for maintaining energy levels throughout the day.

Nutritional Values: Calories 210 | Carbs 25 g | Protein 12 g | Fiber 6 g | Fat 8 g | Sugar 18 g

8.3 Cucumber hummus bites

Preparation Time: 10 min | Cooking Time: 0 min | Servings: 2

Ingredients:
- Cucumber: 1 large
- Hummus: 1/2 cup
- Cherry tomatoes: 4, halved
- Fresh parsley: 1 tbsp, chopped
- Olive oil: 1 tsp
- Lemon juice: 1 tsp
- Salt: to taste
- Black pepper: to taste

Instructions:
Step 1: Wash the cucumber thoroughly and slice it into 1/2-inch thick rounds.
Step 2: Scoop a small amount of the center of each cucumber slice to create a small well, being careful not to cut through the bottom.
Step 3: Fill each cucumber well with about 1 teaspoon of hummus.
Step 4: Top each hummus-filled cucumber slice with a cherry tomato half.
Step 5: Drizzle a small amount of olive oil and lemon juice over the cucumber bites.
Step 6: Sprinkle with chopped parsley, salt, and black pepper to taste.

These cucumber hummus bites are a refreshing and nutritious snack, perfect for maintaining energy levels throughout the day. They are quick to prepare and packed with healthy fats, protein, and fiber.

Nutritional Values: Calories 120 | Carbs 15 g | Protein 4 g | Fiber 4 g | Fat 6 g | Sugar 3 g

8.4 Avocado and egg salad

Preparation Time: 10 min | Cooking Time: 10 min | Servings: 2

Ingredients:
- Avocado: 1 large, ripe
- Eggs: 2 large
- Red onion: 1/4 small, finely chopped
- Cherry tomatoes: 1/2 cup, halved
- Fresh cilantro: 2 tablespoons, chopped
- Lime juice: 1 tablespoon
- Olive oil: 1 tablespoon
- Salt: 1/4 teaspoon
- Black pepper: 1/4 teaspoon

Instructions:
Step 1: Hard-boil the eggs by placing them in a pot of boiling water for 9-10 minutes. Once cooked, transfer them to a bowl of ice water to cool.
Step 2: While the eggs are cooling, cut the avocado in half, remove the pit, and scoop the flesh into a mixing bowl. Mash the avocado slightly with a fork, leaving some chunks for texture.
Step 3: Peel the cooled eggs and chop them into bite-sized pieces. Add the chopped eggs to the bowl with the mashed avocado.
Step 4: Add the finely chopped red onion, halved cherry tomatoes, and chopped cilantro to the bowl.
Step 5: Drizzle the lime juice and olive oil over the mixture. Season with salt and black pepper.
Step 6: Gently mix all the ingredients together until well combined. Serve immediately or refrigerate for up to 2 hours before serving.

This avocado and egg salad is a quick and nutritious snack, perfect for maintaining energy levels and managing blood sugar. It's packed with healthy fats, protein, and fresh flavors.

Nutritional Values: Calories 320 | Carbs 12 g | Protein 10 g | Fiber 8 g | Fat 28 g | Sugar 3 g

8.5 Spinach and feta stuffed mushrooms

Preparation Time: 15 min | Cooking Time: 20 min | Servings: 2

Ingredients:
- Large mushrooms: 8 (stems removed)
- Fresh spinach: 2 cups (chopped)
- Feta cheese: 1/2 cup (crumbled)
- Olive oil: 2 tbsp
- Garlic: 2 cloves (minced)
- Onion: 1/4 cup (finely chopped)
- Salt: 1/4 tsp
- Black pepper: 1/4 tsp
- Lemon juice: 1 tbsp

- Fresh parsley: 1 tbsp (chopped, for garnish)

Instructions:
Step 1: Preheat your oven to 375°F (190°C).
Step 2: Heat 1 tbsp of olive oil in a skillet over medium heat. Add the chopped onion and garlic, and sauté until translucent, about 3 minutes.
Step 3: Add the chopped spinach to the skillet and cook until wilted, about 2-3 minutes. Remove from heat and let cool slightly.
Step 4: In a mixing bowl, combine the cooked spinach mixture with crumbled feta cheese. Season with salt, black pepper, and lemon juice. Mix well.
Step 5: Brush the mushroom caps with the remaining olive oil and place them on a baking sheet.
Step 6: Spoon the spinach and feta mixture into each mushroom cap, pressing gently to fill them.
Step 7: Bake in the preheated oven for 15-20 minutes, or until the mushrooms are tender and the filling is heated through.
Step 8: Garnish with chopped fresh parsley before serving.

These spinach and feta stuffed mushrooms are a delightful and nutritious snack, perfect for maintaining energy levels and managing blood sugar. They are quick to prepare and packed with flavor.

Nutritional Values: Calories 150 | Carb 6 g | Protein 7 g | Fiber 2 g | Fat 11 g | Sugar 2 g

8.6 Low-carb blueberry muffins

Preparation Time: 10 min | Cooking Time: 20 min | Servings: 2

Ingredients:
- Almond flour: 1 cup
- Coconut flour: 2 tablespoons
- Baking powder: 1/2 teaspoon
- Salt: 1/4 teaspoon
- Erythritol: 1/4 cup
- Eggs: 2 large
- Unsweetened almond milk: 1/4 cup
- Vanilla extract: 1 teaspoon
- Fresh blueberries: 1/2 cup

Instructions:
Step 1: Preheat your oven to 350°F (175°C) and line a muffin tin with 4 paper liners.
Step 2: In a medium bowl, combine almond flour, coconut flour, baking powder, salt, and erythritol.
Step 3: In another bowl, whisk together the eggs, almond milk, and vanilla extract until well combined.
Step 4: Gradually add the wet ingredients to the dry ingredients, mixing until just combined.
Step 5: Gently fold in the fresh blueberries.
Step 6: Divide the batter evenly among the 4 muffin liners.
Step 7: Bake for 18-20 minutes, or until a toothpick inserted into the center of a muffin comes out clean.
Step 8: Allow the muffins to cool in the tin for 5 minutes before transferring them to a wire rack to cool completely.

These low-carb blueberry muffins are a delicious and nutritious snack, perfect for maintaining energy levels while managing blood sugar. Quick and easy to make, they are ideal for a healthy lifestyle.

Nutritional Values: Calories 150 | Carb 6 g | Protein 6 g | Fiber 3 g | Fat 12 g | Sugar 2 g

8.7 Spicy roasted chickpeas

Preparation Time: 10 min | Cooking Time: 30 min | Servings: 2

Ingredients:
- Chickpeas (canned, drained and rinsed): 1 can (15 oz)
- Olive oil: 1 tbsp
- Paprika: 1 tsp
- Cumin: 1/2 tsp
- Garlic powder: 1/2 tsp
- Cayenne pepper: 1/4 tsp (optional, for extra heat)
- Salt: 1/4 tsp
- Black pepper: 1/4 tsp

Instructions:
Step 1: Preheat your oven to 400°F (200°C). Line a baking sheet with parchment paper.
Step 2: Spread the drained and rinsed chickpeas on a clean kitchen towel and pat them dry. Removing as much moisture as possible will help them become crispier.
Step 3: In a mixing bowl, combine the chickpeas, olive oil, paprika, cumin, garlic powder, cayenne pepper (if using), salt, and black pepper. Toss until the chickpeas are evenly coated with the spices.
Step 4: Spread the seasoned chickpeas in a single layer on the prepared baking sheet.
Step 5: Roast in the preheated oven for 25-30 minutes, stirring halfway through, until the chickpeas are golden and crispy.
Step 6: Remove from the oven and let cool slightly before serving.

This snack is not only delicious but also packed with protein and fiber, making it an excellent choice for maintaining energy levels throughout the day.

Nutritional Values: Calories 180 | Carbs 28 g | Protein 8 g | Fiber 6 g | Fat 6 g | Sugar 0 g

8.8 Coconut and almond energy balls

Preparation Time: 15 min | Cooking Time: 0 min | Servings: 2

Ingredients:
- Medjool dates: 1/2 cup (pitted)
- Almonds: 1/4 cup (raw)
- Shredded coconut: 1/4 cup (unsweetened)
- Almond butter: 2 tablespoons

- Chia seeds: 1 tablespoon
- Vanilla extract: 1/2 teaspoon
- Sea salt: a pinch

Instructions:
Step 1: In a food processor, combine the Medjool dates and raw almonds. Pulse until they are finely chopped and well combined.
Step 2: Add the shredded coconut, almond butter, chia seeds, vanilla extract, and a pinch of sea salt to the mixture. Pulse again until the mixture starts to come together and form a dough-like consistency.
Step 3: Scoop out small portions of the mixture and roll them into balls using your hands. You should get about 6-8 energy balls.
Step 4: Place the energy balls on a plate and refrigerate for at least 30 minutes to firm up before serving.

These coconut and almond energy balls are a perfect snack to keep your energy levels up throughout the day. They are packed with healthy fats, protein, and fiber, making them a nutritious and satisfying option.

Nutritional Values: Calories 220 | Carb 28 g | Protein 5 g | Fiber 6 g | Fat 11 g | Sugar 19 g

8.9 Turkey and cheese roll-ups

Preparation Time: 10 min | Cooking Time: 0 min | Servings: 2

Ingredients:
- Turkey breast slices: 4 oz (approximately 4 slices)
- Low-fat cheese slices: 2 oz (approximately 2 slices)
- Avocado: 1/2, sliced
- Baby spinach leaves: 1 cup
- Whole grain mustard: 2 tsp
- Whole wheat tortillas: 2 medium-sized

Instructions:
Step 1: Lay the whole wheat tortillas flat on a clean surface.
Step 2: Spread 1 tsp of whole grain mustard evenly over each tortilla.
Step 3: Place 2 slices of turkey breast on each tortilla.
Step 4: Add 1 slice of low-fat cheese on top of the turkey.
Step 5: Arrange avocado slices and baby spinach leaves evenly over the cheese.
Step 6: Roll up the tortillas tightly, ensuring all ingredients are enclosed.
Step 7: Slice each roll-up into bite-sized pieces or serve whole.

These turkey and cheese roll-ups are a quick and nutritious snack, perfect for maintaining energy levels throughout the day. They are easy to prepare and packed with protein and healthy fats.

Nutritional Values: Calories 250 | Carbs 20 g | Protein 18 g | Fiber 6 g | Fat 12 g | Sugar 2 g

8.10 Green apple and peanut butter slices

Preparation Time: 10 min | **Cooking Time:** 0 min | **Servings:** 2

Ingredients:
- Green apples: 2 medium
- Peanut butter: 4 tablespoons
- Chia seeds: 1 teaspoon
- Cinnamon: 1/2 teaspoon
- Honey: 1 teaspoon (optional)

Instructions:
Step 1: Wash and core the green apples. Slice each apple into 1/4-inch thick rings.
Step 2: Spread 1 tablespoon of peanut butter evenly on each apple slice.
Step 3: Sprinkle chia seeds and cinnamon over the peanut butter.
Step 4: Drizzle a small amount of honey over the top of each slice if desired.

This snack is a perfect blend of crunch and creaminess, providing a quick energy boost with healthy fats and proteins. It's easy to make and ideal for maintaining stable blood sugar levels.

Nutritional Values: Calories 210 | Carbs 28 g | Protein 6 g | Fiber 7 g | Fat 11 g | Sugar 18 g

8.11 Flaxseed and walnut crackers

Preparation Time: 10 min | **Cooking Time:** 15 min | **Servings:** 2

Ingredients:
- Ground flaxseed: 1/2 cup
- Walnut pieces: 1/2 cup
- Water: 1/4 cup
- Olive oil: 1 tbsp
- Salt: 1/4 tsp
- Garlic powder: 1/4 tsp
- Onion powder: 1/4 tsp

Instructions:
Step 1: Preheat the oven to 350°F (175°C) and line a baking sheet with parchment paper.
Step 2: In a food processor, blend the walnut pieces until they are finely ground.
Step 3: In a mixing bowl, combine the ground flaxseed, ground walnuts, salt, garlic powder, and onion powder.
Step 4: Add the water and olive oil to the dry ingredients and mix until a dough forms.
Step 5: Place the dough between two sheets of parchment paper and roll it out to about 1/8 inch thickness.
Step 6: Remove the top sheet of parchment paper and cut the dough into cracker-sized pieces using a knife or pizza cutter.
Step 7: Transfer the parchment paper with the cut dough onto the baking sheet.
Step 8: Bake for 12-15 minutes, or until the edges are golden brown and the crackers are crisp.
Step 9: Allow the crackers to cool completely on the baking sheet before breaking them apart.

These flaxseed and walnut crackers are a perfect snack for maintaining energy levels and managing blood sugar. They are quick to prepare and packed with healthy fats and fiber.

Nutritional Values: Calories 220 | Carbs 8 g | Protein 6 g | Fiber 6 g | Fat 18 g | Sugar 0 g

8.12 Zucchini and parmesan chips

Preparation Time: 10 min | Cooking Time: 10 min | Servings: 2

Ingredients:
- Zucchini: 1 medium
- Parmesan cheese: 1/2 cup, grated
- Olive oil: 1 tbsp
- Garlic powder: 1/2 tsp
- Salt: 1/4 tsp
- Black pepper: 1/4 tsp

Instructions:
Step 1: Preheat your oven to 425°F (220°C) and line a baking sheet with parchment paper.
Step 2: Slice the zucchini into thin rounds, about 1/8 inch thick.
Step 3: In a bowl, toss the zucchini slices with olive oil, garlic powder, salt, and black pepper until evenly coated.
Step 4: Arrange the zucchini slices in a single layer on the prepared baking sheet.
Step 5: Sprinkle the grated Parmesan cheese evenly over the zucchini slices.
Step 6: Bake in the preheated oven for 10-15 minutes, or until the zucchini is crispy and the cheese is golden brown.
Step 7: Remove from the oven and let cool for a few minutes before serving.

These zucchini and parmesan chips are a delicious and healthy snack option, perfect for maintaining energy levels and managing blood sugar. They are quick to prepare and packed with flavor.

Nutritional Values: Calories 150 | Carbs 5 g | Protein 8 g | Fiber 1 g | Fat 11 g | Sugar 2 g

8.13 Bell pepper and guacamole boats

Preparation Time: 10 min | Cooking Time: 10 min | Servings: 2

Ingredients:
- Bell peppers: 2 medium (any color)
- Ripe avocados: 2
- Red onion: 1/4 cup, finely chopped
- Cherry tomatoes: 1/2 cup, diced
- Cilantro: 2 tablespoons, chopped
- Lime: 1, juiced
- Salt: 1/2 teaspoon

- Black pepper: 1/4 teaspoon
- Olive oil: 1 teaspoon (optional)

Instructions:
Step 1: Cut the bell peppers in half lengthwise and remove the seeds and membranes.
Step 2: In a medium bowl, mash the avocados until smooth.
Step 3: Add the finely chopped red onion, diced cherry tomatoes, chopped cilantro, lime juice, salt, and black pepper to the mashed avocados. Mix well.
Step 4: Fill each bell pepper half with the guacamole mixture.
Step 5: Drizzle with olive oil if desired.
Step 6: Serve immediately or refrigerate for up to 1 hour before serving.

This dish is a quick and easy snack that is packed with healthy fats, vitamins, and minerals. Perfect for maintaining energy levels and managing blood sugar.

Nutritional Values: Calories 220 | Carb 18 g | Protein 3 g | Fiber 11 g | Fat 18 g | Sugar 5 g

8.14 Cottage cheese and cherry tomatoes

Preparation Time: 10 min | Cooking Time: 10 min | Servings: 2

Ingredients:
- Cottage cheese: 1 cup
- Cherry tomatoes: 1 cup, halved
- Fresh basil: 1 tablespoon, chopped
- Olive oil: 1 tablespoon
- Salt: 1/4 teaspoon
- Black pepper: 1/4 teaspoon
- Balsamic vinegar: 1 teaspoon (optional)

Instructions:
Step 1: In a medium bowl, combine the cottage cheese, halved cherry tomatoes, and chopped fresh basil.
Step 2: Drizzle the olive oil over the mixture and season with salt and black pepper.
Step 3: Gently toss all ingredients until well combined. If desired, add a splash of balsamic vinegar for extra flavor.
Step 4: Serve immediately or refrigerate for up to 2 hours before serving.

This dish is a perfect blend of creamy cottage cheese and juicy cherry tomatoes, providing a refreshing and nutritious snack that is quick and easy to prepare. It's ideal for maintaining energy levels and managing blood sugar.

Nutritional Values: Calories 150 | Carbs 10 g | Protein 14 g | Fiber 2 g | Fat 8 g | Sugar 6 g

8.15 Smoked salmon and cream cheese cucumber rolls

Preparation Time: 15 min | Cooking Time: 0 min | Servings: 2

Ingredients:
- Cucumber: 1 large
- Smoked salmon: 4 oz
- Cream cheese: 4 tbsp
- Fresh dill: 1 tbsp, chopped
- Lemon juice: 1 tsp
- Black pepper: to taste

Instructions:
Step 1: Slice the cucumber lengthwise into thin strips using a mandoline or a sharp knife.
Step 2: In a small bowl, mix the cream cheese, chopped dill, lemon juice, and black pepper until well combined.
Step 3: Lay out a cucumber strip and spread a thin layer of the cream cheese mixture over it.
Step 4: Place a slice of smoked salmon on top of the cream cheese.
Step 5: Carefully roll up the cucumber strip and secure it with a toothpick if necessary.
Step 6: Repeat with the remaining cucumber strips, cream cheese mixture, and smoked salmon.
Step 7: Arrange the rolls on a serving platter and garnish with extra dill if desired.

These smoked salmon and cream cheese cucumber rolls are a refreshing and nutritious snack, perfect for maintaining energy levels while managing blood sugar. They are quick to prepare and packed with protein and healthy fats.

Nutritional Values: Calories 150 | Carbs 6 g | Protein 12 g | Fiber 1 g | Fat 10 g | Sugar 3 g

8.16 Baked kale chips

Preparation Time: 10 min | Cooking Time: 10 min | Servings: 2

Ingredients:
- Kale: 1 bunch (about 6 oz)
- Olive oil: 1 tbsp
- Sea salt: 1/2 tsp
- Garlic powder: 1/4 tsp (optional)
- Paprika: 1/4 tsp (optional)

Instructions:
Step 1: Preheat your oven to 350°F (175°C).
Step 2: Wash and thoroughly dry the kale leaves. Remove the tough stems and tear the leaves into bite-sized pieces.
Step 3: In a large bowl, drizzle the kale with olive oil and sprinkle with sea salt, garlic powder, and paprika. Toss to coat evenly.
Step 4: Spread the kale leaves in a single layer on a baking sheet lined with parchment paper.
Step 5: Bake in the preheated oven for 10-15 minutes, or until the edges are brown but not burnt. Keep an eye

on them to prevent overcooking.
Step 6: Remove from the oven and let cool for a few minutes before serving.

Kale chips are a delicious, crispy snack that is packed with nutrients and perfect for maintaining energy levels throughout the day. They are quick to make and a great alternative to traditional chips.

Nutritional Values: Calories 70 | Carbs 7 g | Protein 3 g | Fiber 2 g | Fat 4 g | Sugar 0 g

8.17 Peanut butter and banana smoothie

Preparation Time: 5 min | Cooking Time: 0 min | Servings: 2

Ingredients:
- Banana: 2 medium, ripe
- Peanut butter: 2 tablespoons
- Greek yogurt: 1 cup, plain
- Almond milk: 1 cup, unsweetened
- Honey: 1 tablespoon (optional)
- Ice cubes: 1 cup

Instructions:
Step 1: Peel the bananas and cut them into chunks.
Step 2: Add the banana chunks, peanut butter, Greek yogurt, almond milk, and honey (if using) into a blender.
Step 3: Add the ice cubes to the blender.
Step 4: Blend on high speed until smooth and creamy.
Step 5: Pour the smoothie into two glasses and serve immediately.

This smoothie is a delicious and quick way to boost your energy levels. It's packed with protein, healthy fats, and natural sugars, making it an ideal snack for maintaining energy throughout the day.

Nutritional Values: Calories 270 | Carbs 35 g | Protein 12 g | Fiber 4 g | Fat 11 g | Sugar 20 g

8.18 Grilled vegetable kebabs

Preparation Time: 15 min | Cooking Time: 10 min | Servings: 2

Ingredients:
- Bell peppers (red, yellow, green): 1 cup, chopped
- Zucchini: 1 medium, sliced
- Red onion: 1 small, cut into wedges
- Cherry tomatoes: 1 cup
- Olive oil: 2 tablespoons
- Garlic powder: 1 teaspoon
- Dried oregano: 1 teaspoon
- Salt: 1/2 teaspoon

- Black pepper: 1/4 teaspoon
- Lemon juice: 1 tablespoon
- Wooden skewers: 4-6, soaked in water for 30 minutes

Instructions:
Step 1: Preheat the grill to medium-high heat.
Step 2: In a large bowl, combine the bell peppers, zucchini, red onion, and cherry tomatoes.
Step 3: In a small bowl, whisk together the olive oil, garlic powder, dried oregano, salt, black pepper, and lemon juice.
Step 4: Pour the olive oil mixture over the vegetables and toss to coat evenly.
Step 5: Thread the vegetables onto the soaked wooden skewers, alternating the types of vegetables.
Step 6: Place the skewers on the preheated grill and cook for 8-10 minutes, turning occasionally, until the vegetables are tender and slightly charred.
Step 7: Remove from the grill and serve immediately.

These grilled vegetable kebabs are a quick and nutritious snack that is perfect for maintaining energy levels. The colorful mix of vegetables provides a variety of vitamins and minerals, making it a healthy choice for any time of the day.

Nutritional Values: Calories 120 | Carb 15 g | Protein 3 g | Fiber 4 g | Fat 7 g | Sugar 7 g

SCAN THE QR CODE
TO ACCESS
YOUR EXCLUSIVE BONUS
info@retoteufel.com

9. 4-week meal plan for diabetes management

As a professional chef and dietician, I have crafted a balanced and nutritious 4-week meal plan for Sarah, a dedicated mother and high school teacher recently diagnosed with Type 2 diabetes. This meal plan is designed to help Sarah manage her diabetes effectively while ensuring her meals are both delicious and family-friendly. Each day includes breakfast, lunch, dinner, and snacks, using the provided recipes to create a varied and enjoyable diet.

Week 1

Monday:
- Breakfast: Oatmeal with chia and berries
- Lunch: Turkey and avocado wrap
- Dinner: Grilled chicken caesar salad
- Snacks: Almond and pumpkin seed mix

Tuesday:
- Breakfast: Spinach and feta egg muffins
- Lunch: Quinoa and black bean salad
- Dinner: Baked salmon with steamed broccoli
- Snacks: Cucumber hummus bites

Wednesday:
- Breakfast: Almond butter smoothie
- Lunch: Vegetable lentil soup
- Dinner: Beef and vegetable stir-fry
- Snacks: Low-carb blueberry muffins

Thursday:
- Breakfast: Cottage cheese and peach parfait
- Lunch: Spinach and feta stuffed chicken
- Dinner: Zucchini noodle and shrimp bowl
- Snacks: Green apple and peanut butter slices

Friday:
- Breakfast: Quinoa and apple breakfast bowl
- Lunch: Mediterranean chickpea wrap
- Dinner: Turkey chili
- Snacks: Spicy roasted chickpeas

Saturday:
- Breakfast: Greek yogurt with nuts and honey
- Lunch: Tuna salad stuffed tomatoes
- Dinner: Spaghetti squash with turkey meatballs
- Snacks: Smoked salmon and cream cheese cucumber rolls

Sunday:
- Breakfast: Tofu scramble with vegetables
- Lunch: Balsamic chicken and roasted vegetable salad
- Dinner: Chicken tikka masala with cauliflower
- Snacks: Coconut and almond energy balls

Week 2

Monday:
- Breakfast: Buckwheat pancakes
- Lunch: Grilled chicken with quinoa salad
- Dinner: Vegetarian chili
- Snacks: Cottage cheese and cherry tomatoes

Tuesday:
- Breakfast: Chia pudding with coconut milk
- Lunch: Roasted vegetable and hummus wrap
- Dinner: Lentil and mushroom stew
- Snacks: Bell pepper and guacamole boats

Wednesday:
- Breakfast: Smoked salmon and cream cheese bagel
- Lunch: Asian chicken salad
- Dinner: Baked cod with olive tapenade
- Snacks: Turkey and cheese roll-ups

Thursday:
- Breakfast: Kale and sweet potato hash
- Lunch: Egg salad on rye
- Dinner: Stuffed acorn squash
- Snacks: Peanut butter and banana smoothie

Friday:
- Breakfast: Blueberry and almond oat bars
- Lunch: Caprese salad with grilled chicken
- Dinner: Chicken and barley soup
- Snacks: Zucchini and parmesan chips

Saturday:
- Breakfast: Ricotta and pear toast
- Lunch: Mediterranean chickpea salad
- Dinner: Pork tenderloin with apple cider glaze
- Snacks: Flaxseed and walnut crackers

Sunday:
- Breakfast: Vegetable omelette
- Lunch: Beetroot and goat cheese salad

- Dinner: Grilled vegetable platter with herb dressing
- Snacks: Baked kale chips

Week 3

Monday:
- Breakfast: Protein-packed breakfast tacos
- Lunch: Turkey and spinach stuffed peppers
- Dinner: Tofu and vegetable curry
- Snacks: Chia and berry yogurt parfait

Tuesday:
- Breakfast: Banana and walnut bread
- Lunch: Broccoli and cheddar stuffed potatoes
- Dinner: Eggplant and chickpea tagine
- Snacks: Spinach and feta stuffed mushrooms

Wednesday:
- Breakfast: Green detox smoothie
- Lunch: Tuna and white bean salad
- Dinner: Chicken tortilla soup
- Snacks: Grilled vegetable kebabs

Thursday:
- Breakfast: Turkey and avocado wrap
- Lunch: Roasted turkey with garlic green beans
- Dinner: Cauliflower rice and shrimp bowl
- Snacks: Avocado and egg salad

Friday:
- Breakfast: Quinoa and apple breakfast bowl
- Lunch: Smoked salmon and arugula salad
- Dinner: Split pea and ham soup
- Snacks: Spicy roasted chickpeas

Saturday:
- Breakfast: Greek yogurt with nuts and honey
- Lunch: Buffalo chicken salad
- Dinner: Mushroom and thyme soup
- Snacks: Coconut and almond energy balls

Sunday:
- Breakfast: Tofu scramble with vegetables
- Lunch: Pear and blue cheese salad
- Dinner: Chicken tikka masala with cauliflower
- Snacks: Turkey and cheese roll-ups

Week 4

Monday:
- Breakfast: Buckwheat pancakes
- Lunch: Grilled chicken with quinoa salad
- Dinner: Vegetarian chili
- Snacks: Cottage cheese and cherry tomatoes

Tuesday:
- Breakfast: Chia pudding with coconut milk
- Lunch: Roasted vegetable and hummus wrap
- Dinner: Lentil and mushroom stew
- Snacks: Bell pepper and guacamole boats

Wednesday:
- Breakfast: Smoked salmon and cream cheese bagel
- Lunch: Asian chicken salad
- Dinner: Baked cod with olive tapenade
- Snacks: Turkey and cheese roll-ups

Thursday:
- Breakfast: Kale and sweet potato hash
- Lunch: Egg salad on rye
- Dinner: Stuffed acorn squash
- Snacks: Peanut butter and banana smoothie

Friday:
- Breakfast: Blueberry and almond oat bars
- Lunch: Caprese salad with grilled chicken
- Dinner: Chicken and barley soup
- Snacks: Zucchini and parmesan chips

Saturday:
- Breakfast: Ricotta and pear toast
- Lunch: Mediterranean chickpea salad
- Dinner: Pork tenderloin with apple cider glaze
- Snacks: Flaxseed and walnut crackers

Sunday:
- Breakfast: Vegetable omelette
- Lunch: Beetroot and goat cheese salad
- Dinner: Grilled vegetable platter with herb dressing
- Snacks: Baked kale chips

10. Conclusion: embracing a healthy lifestyle

Embracing a healthy lifestyle is not just a goal but a journey that requires dedication, patience, and a positive mindset. As we conclude this comprehensive guide on the diabetic diet, it is essential to reflect on the key points discussed throughout the book and understand how they collectively contribute to managing diabetes effectively. The foundation of a balanced diabetic diet lies in understanding the role of macronutrients—carbohydrates, proteins, and fats—and how they impact blood sugar levels.

By choosing the right types of carbohydrates, such as whole grains, legumes, and vegetables, you can ensure a steady release of glucose into the bloodstream, preventing spikes and crashes. Incorporating high-fiber foods helps in slowing down digestion and absorption, further aiding in blood sugar control. Proteins play a crucial role in maintaining muscle mass and providing satiety, while healthy fats, such as those found in avocados, nuts, and olive oil, support heart health and provide essential fatty acids.

Reading and understanding food labels is another critical skill that empowers you to make informed choices. By paying attention to serving sizes, carbohydrate content, and added sugars, you can better manage your dietary intake and avoid hidden sources of sugar. The book has provided a variety of delicious and nutritious recipes for every meal of the day, from hearty breakfasts to satisfying lunches and dinners, as well as flavorful salads, soothing soups, and energy-boosting snacks. Each recipe is designed to balance macronutrients, incorporate nutrient-dense ingredients, and cater to diverse tastes and preferences. For instance, starting your day with oatmeal with chia and berries or a spinach and feta egg muffin can provide a nutritious and energizing breakfast. Lunch options like a quinoa and black bean salad or a grilled chicken Caesar salad offer a mix of proteins, healthy fats, and fiber to keep you full and satisfied. Dinner recipes such as grilled chicken with quinoa salad or baked salmon with steamed broccoli ensure you end your day with a balanced and wholesome meal.

Maintaining a healthy lifestyle goes beyond just following a diet; it involves integrating these healthy habits into your daily routine. Meal planning and preparation are essential strategies to stay on track. By dedicating time each week to plan your meals, create a shopping list, and prepare ingredients in advance, you can reduce the stress and time associated with daily cooking. Batch cooking and storing meals in portioned containers can also help you manage your time efficiently and ensure you always have a healthy option available. Staying motivated in your diet journey is crucial, and one way to do this is by setting realistic and achievable goals. Celebrate small victories, such as successfully trying a new recipe or maintaining stable blood sugar levels, and use these accomplishments as motivation to continue. Engaging with a support system, whether through diabetes support groups, online communities, or family and friends, can provide encouragement and accountability. Sharing your experiences, challenges, and successes with others who understand your journey can make a significant difference in staying committed to your health goals.

Incorporating physical activity into your daily routine is another vital aspect of a healthy lifestyle. Regular exercise helps improve insulin sensitivity, manage weight, and reduce the risk of complications associated with diabetes. Find activities you enjoy, whether it's walking, swimming, cycling, or yoga, and aim for at least 150 minutes of moderate-intensity exercise per week. Remember that staying active doesn't have to be a chore; it can be a fun and rewarding part of your day. Reflecting on your journey and acknowledging the progress you've made is essential. Take time to assess what has worked well for you and what areas may need improvement. Use this reflection to adjust your strategies and set new goals. Embracing a healthy lifestyle is an ongoing process, and it's important to be kind to yourself and recognize that setbacks may occur. What matters most is your commitment to getting back on track and continuing to make positive choices.

As you move forward, continue to educate yourself about diabetes management and stay informed about new research and recommendations. Subscribe to health and wellness newsletters, follow food bloggers who specialize in diabetic-friendly recipes, and participate in health workshops or cooking classes. Staying engaged and informed will help you stay motivated and empowered in your journey. In conclusion, embracing a healthy lifestyle with a balanced diabetic diet is a powerful tool in managing diabetes and improving your overall quality of life. By understanding the role of macronutrients, reading food labels, planning and preparing meals, staying motivated, incorporating physical activity, and reflecting on your journey, you can achieve your health goals and enjoy a fulfilling and vibrant life. Remember that you are not alone in this journey, and with the right knowledge, support, and determination, you can successfully navigate the complexities of diabetic nutrition and thrive.

10.1 Reflecting on your journey

Reflecting on your journey with diabetes is an essential part of embracing a healthy lifestyle and maintaining the motivation to continue making positive changes. As you look back on the path you've traveled, it's important to acknowledge the challenges you've faced, the progress you've made, and the lessons you've learned along the way. This reflection not only helps you appreciate your achievements but also reinforces the importance of the dietary changes you've implemented and their impact on your overall health and well-being.

When Sarah, a dedicated mother and high school teacher, was first diagnosed with Type 2 diabetes, she felt overwhelmed and uncertain about how to manage her condition. Like many others, she struggled to understand the complexities of diabetic nutrition and often found herself frustrated by the conflicting information available. However, Sarah's commitment to improving her health and preventing complications motivated her to seek out reliable resources and support. She joined diabetes support groups, attended health workshops, and subscribed to health and wellness newsletters. Through these efforts, Sarah discovered the "Diabetic Diet Cookbook for Beginners," which became a valuable tool in her journey toward better health.

Reflecting on her journey, Sarah recalls the initial challenges she faced in understanding food labels and finding recipes that met her dietary needs while still being appealing to her family. Meal planning and preparation were time-consuming, especially with her busy schedule as a teacher and mother. However, the comprehensive guide provided by the cookbook helped her navigate these complexities. The book's detailed explanations of macronutrients, the importance of carbohydrates and fiber, and the role of proteins and fats in a diabetic diet gave her the knowledge she needed to make informed food choices.

Sarah also found inspiration in the personal stories shared within the cookbook. Reading about others who had successfully managed their diabetes through dietary changes gave her hope and motivation. For example, she was particularly moved by the story of John, a retired engineer who had struggled with diabetes for years before discovering the benefits of a balanced diet. John's story highlighted the positive impact of incorporating more whole grains, lean proteins, and healthy fats into his meals. He shared how these changes not only helped him manage his blood sugar levels but also improved his overall energy and quality of life.

As Sarah implemented the dietary changes recommended in the cookbook, she began to notice significant improvements in her health. Her blood sugar levels stabilized, she lost weight, and she felt more energetic and focused throughout the day. These positive outcomes reinforced her commitment to maintaining a balanced diabetic diet. Sarah also took pride in the fact that her family benefited from the healthier meals she prepared. Her children enjoyed the nutritious and delicious recipes, and her husband appreciated the variety of flavors and ingredients.

Reflecting on her journey, Sarah recognizes the importance of setting realistic goals and celebrating small victories. She recalls the satisfaction she felt when she successfully prepared her first diabetic-friendly meal, a quinoa and black bean salad, which quickly became a family favorite. This sense of accomplishment motivated her to continue experimenting with new recipes and ingredients. Over time, Sarah developed a repertoire of go-to meals that were both nutritious and enjoyable.

Sarah's journey also taught her the value of self-compassion and patience. There were times when she felt discouraged, especially when faced with setbacks or when her progress seemed slow. However, she learned to view these moments as opportunities for growth and reflection. By focusing on the positive changes she had made and the progress she had achieved, Sarah was able to stay motivated and continue moving forward.

Research supports the importance of reflection in maintaining long-term dietary changes. A study published in the journal "Diabetes Care" found that individuals who regularly reflected on their dietary habits and progress were more likely to adhere to a healthy eating plan and achieve better glycemic control. The study emphasized the role of self-monitoring and reflection in fostering a sense of accountability and motivation.

In addition to personal reflection, Sarah found it helpful to engage with online communities and support groups focused on diabetes management. These platforms provided a space for her to share her experiences, seek advice, and connect with others who understood the challenges of living with diabetes. Through these interactions, Sarah gained valuable insights and tips for managing her condition. For example, she learned about the benefits of meal prepping and how it could save time and reduce stress during busy weekdays. She also discovered new recipes and cooking techniques that made healthy eating more enjoyable and sustainable.

Reflecting on her journey, Sarah is grateful for the support and resources that have helped her along the way. The "Diabetic Diet Cookbook for Beginners" played a crucial role in providing her with the knowledge and tools she needed to make positive changes. The personal stories, practical tips, and delicious recipes within the book empowered her to take control of her health and embrace a balanced diabetic diet.

As you reflect on your own journey, consider the progress you've made and the positive changes you've implemented. Acknowledge the challenges you've faced and the lessons you've learned. Celebrate your achievements, no matter how small, and use them as motivation to continue moving forward. Remember that managing diabetes is a lifelong journey, and every step you take toward a healthier lifestyle is a step in the right direction.

Reflecting on your journey also involves recognizing the impact of your dietary changes on your overall well-being. Consider how your energy levels, mood, and physical health have improved since you began following a balanced diabetic diet. Take note of the positive changes in your blood sugar levels, weight, and other health markers. These improvements are a testament to your dedication and commitment to your health.

As you continue on your journey, remember that you are not alone. Many others, like Sarah, have faced similar challenges and have found success through perseverance and support. By reflecting on your journey and staying motivated, you can continue to make positive changes and achieve your health goals. Embrace the lessons you've learned, celebrate your progress, and look forward to a healthier and more fulfilling future.

10.2 Staying motivated in your diet journey

Staying motivated in your diet journey is a crucial aspect of successfully managing diabetes through dietary changes. It's not uncommon for individuals, including our ideal reader Sarah, to face challenges in maintaining motivation and commitment to a diabetic-friendly diet. However, with the right strategies and mindset, it is entirely possible to stay inspired and dedicated to this healthy lifestyle. One of the first steps in staying motivated is to set realistic and achievable goals. These goals should be specific, measurable, attainable, relevant, and time-bound (SMART). For example, Sarah might set a goal to reduce her HbA1c levels by a certain percentage within six months or to incorporate at least three new diabetic-friendly recipes into her weekly meal plan. By setting clear and attainable goals, Sarah can track her progress and celebrate her achievements, which can provide a significant motivational boost.

Another effective strategy is to create a supportive environment. This includes involving family and friends in the journey. Sarah can educate her family about the importance of a diabetic diet and encourage them to join her in making healthier food choices. This not only provides her with a support system but also ensures that the entire household benefits from nutritious meals. Additionally, Sarah can join diabetes support groups, either in-person or online, where she can share her experiences, seek advice, and gain inspiration from others who are on a similar journey. These communities can offer valuable emotional support and practical tips for staying motivated.

Meal planning and preparation can also play a significant role in maintaining motivation. By dedicating time each week to plan meals and prepare ingredients, Sarah can reduce the stress and time associated with daily cooking. This can make it easier to stick to a diabetic-friendly diet, even on busy days. Sarah can also experiment with new recipes and cooking techniques to keep her meals exciting and prevent dietary boredom. For instance, she might try a new spice blend or cooking method, such as grilling or steaming, to add variety to her meals. Incorporating seasonal produce can also add freshness and diversity to her diet.

Overcoming common challenges, such as social dining, is another important aspect of staying motivated. Social events and dining out can be particularly challenging for individuals following a diabetic diet. However, with some planning and communication, Sarah can navigate these situations successfully. When dining out, she can review the menu in advance and choose dishes that align with her dietary needs. She can also communicate her dietary restrictions to the restaurant staff to ensure her meal is prepared accordingly. When attending social events, Sarah can bring a diabetic-friendly dish to share, ensuring there is at least one option that meets her dietary requirements. This not only helps her stay on track but also introduces others to delicious and healthy diabetic-friendly foods.

Staying inspired in the kitchen is essential for maintaining motivation. Sarah can draw inspiration from various sources, such as cookbooks, food blogs, and cooking shows that focus on diabetic-friendly recipes. She can also attend cooking classes or workshops to learn new skills and techniques. Experimenting with different cuisines and flavors can make meal preparation an enjoyable and creative process. For example, Sarah might explore Mediterranean or Asian-inspired dishes, which often include a variety of vegetables, lean proteins, and healthy fats that are suitable for a diabetic diet.

In addition to these strategies, it's important for Sarah to practice self-compassion and patience. Managing diabetes through diet is a journey, and there may be setbacks along the way. It's essential for Sarah to recognize that perfection is not the goal and that occasional indulgences or slip-ups are part of the process. By focusing on her overall progress and maintaining a positive mindset, Sarah can stay motivated and committed to her diabetic diet.

Research supports the importance of motivation in managing diabetes. A study published in the journal Diabetes Care found that individuals who set specific dietary goals and received support from their social network were more likely to adhere to their diabetic diet and achieve better health outcomes. Another study highlighted the role of self-efficacy, or the belief in one's ability to succeed, in maintaining dietary changes. By building confidence in her ability to manage her diet, Sarah can enhance her motivation and commitment.

In conclusion, staying motivated in your diet journey requires a combination of goal-setting, creating a supportive environment, meal planning, overcoming challenges, and finding inspiration in the kitchen. By implementing these strategies, Sarah can maintain her motivation and commitment to a diabetic-friendly diet, ultimately improving her overall health and well-being. This journey is not just about managing diabetes; it's about embracing a healthier lifestyle that benefits both Sarah and her family. By staying motivated and dedicated, Sarah can achieve her health goals and enjoy a fulfilling and nutritious diet.

10.3 Integrating healthy habits into daily life

Integrating healthy habits into daily life is a cornerstone of managing diabetes effectively and ensuring long-term well-being. As you embark on this journey, it's essential to understand that small, consistent changes can lead to significant improvements in your health. The principles of a diabetic diet, as discussed throughout this book, are not just temporary measures but should be seamlessly woven into the fabric of your everyday life. This subchapter will provide practical tips, routines, and strategies to make healthy eating a natural and enjoyable part of your daily activities.

One of the first steps to integrating healthy habits is to establish a routine that works for you and your family. Begin by planning your meals ahead of time. Meal planning can seem daunting at first, but it becomes easier with practice and can save you time and stress in the long run. Start by setting aside a specific day each week to plan your meals, create a shopping list, and prepare some ingredients in advance. For example, you might choose Sunday afternoons to plan your meals for the week, chop vegetables, and cook a few staples like grilled chicken or quinoa. This preparation will make it easier to assemble healthy meals quickly during busy weekdays.

Incorporating a variety of foods into your diet is another key aspect of maintaining a balanced diabetic diet. Aim to include a mix of lean proteins, whole grains, healthy fats, and plenty of fruits and vegetables in your meals. For instance, a typical day might start with a breakfast of oatmeal topped with chia seeds and berries, followed by a lunch of a quinoa and black bean salad, and a dinner of baked salmon with steamed broccoli. Snacks can include options like a handful of almonds or a piece of fruit. By diversifying your diet, you not only ensure that you get a wide range of nutrients but also keep your meals interesting and satisfying.

Understanding portion sizes is crucial for managing blood sugar levels. Use measuring cups and a food scale to familiarize yourself with appropriate portion sizes, especially when you are first starting out. Over time, you will develop a better sense of how much you should be eating. Additionally, try to eat at regular intervals to keep your blood sugar levels stable. Skipping meals or going too long without eating can lead to fluctuations in blood sugar, which can be harmful for individuals with diabetes.

Another practical tip is to make healthy swaps in your favorite recipes. For example, if you love pasta, try using zucchini noodles or spaghetti squash instead of traditional pasta. If you enjoy baking, experiment with using almond flour or coconut flour instead of white flour. These small changes can make a big difference in the nutritional content of your meals without sacrificing flavor. Additionally, look for ways to reduce added sugars in your diet. Opt for natural sweeteners like stevia or monk fruit, and be mindful of hidden sugars in processed foods.

Staying hydrated is also an important aspect of a healthy lifestyle. Aim to drink at least eight glasses of water a day, and consider carrying a reusable water bottle with you to make it easier to stay on track. Herbal teas and infused water with slices of fruit or herbs can add variety and make hydration more enjoyable.

Physical activity is another critical component of managing diabetes and maintaining overall health. Find an exercise routine that you enjoy and can stick with. This could be anything from walking, swimming, or cycling to joining a fitness class or practicing yoga. Aim for at least 150 minutes of moderate-intensity exercise each week, as recommended by the American Diabetes Association. Incorporating physical activity into your daily routine can help improve insulin sensitivity, lower blood sugar levels, and boost your mood and energy levels.

Mindfulness and stress management are also important for overall well-being. Chronic stress can negatively impact blood sugar levels and overall health. Consider incorporating mindfulness practices such as meditation, deep breathing exercises, or journaling into your daily routine. These practices can help you manage stress and stay focused on your health goals.

Involving your family in your healthy lifestyle changes can also make a big difference. Encourage your family members to join you in meal planning, cooking, and exercising. This not only provides support and accountability but also ensures that everyone benefits from healthier habits. For example, you could have a family cooking night where everyone helps prepare a nutritious meal, or plan weekend activities that involve physical exercise, such as hiking or playing a sport together.

It's also important to stay informed and continue learning about diabetes management. Join online communities, attend workshops, and read up-to-date information from reliable sources. Engaging with others who are on a similar journey can provide valuable support and motivation. Additionally, consider working with a registered dietitian or diabetes educator who can provide personalized guidance and help you navigate any challenges you may encounter.

Remember, integrating healthy habits into your daily life is a gradual process. Be patient with yourself and celebrate your progress, no matter how small. Every positive change you make brings you one step closer to better health and well-being. By consistently applying the principles of a diabetic diet and making mindful choices, you can effectively manage your diabetes and enjoy a fulfilling, healthy life.

Made in the USA
Monee, IL
05 February 2025